TABLE OF CONTENTS

PREFACE

INTRODUCTION

- *A Random List of Traitors and Treachery in U.S. History*

    - ✓ *Benedict Arnold*
    - ✓ *Denmark Vesey*
    - ✓ *Anne Savage*
    - ✓ *Elia Kazan*
    - ✓ *Walt Disney*
    - ✓ *Ronald Reagan*
    - ✓ *Michael Fortier*
    - ✓ *Leroy"Nikki" Barnes*
    - ✓ *Jose Canseco*
    - ✓ *Linda Tripp*
    - ✓ *Sammy "The Bull" Gravano*
    - ✓ *Kobe Bryant*
    - ✓ *Jimmy Henchman*

- *Notes and a Primer: Cops, Crime and "The Capture"*
- *"Organized Crime"*

    - ✓ *Organized Crime, Snitching and Young Rapper/Gangster Wannabes*

- *Notes on the Witness Protection Program*
- *Notes on the "Confidential Informant"*

SNITCH: A LONGITUDINAL STUDY

- *1938 – The Omaha Star and it's anti-Snitch/anti-Sellout Message*
- *1959 – The Beginning of COINTELPRO*
- *1960 – COINTELPRO and the Snitches*

  ✓ **Government Snitch: Earl Anthony and His Antics**

- *The Snitch System, 1969-1970 – Omaha is Infiltrated*
- *1981 – Omaha and "Mr. Snitch"*

  ✓ **Petition on Police Brutality - 9-29-81**

- *1982 – Prime Prevention as Aide to Revitalization*
- *1989 – The Rise of "Mad Dads"*
- *1995 – "Law Enforcement Sunday"*
- *2004*

  ✓ *Speech by Sen. Ernie Chambers on DNA Collection and Community Rights*
  ✓ *A Speech by African-American Police Chief Thomas Warren*

CONCLUSION
WORKS CITED

PREFACE

    We've got too many black kids killing each other and it's far too simple and simplistic to pawn it off as "unconscious self-hatred" or "low self-esteem." I believe that at the base of a majority of these murders is the police-controlled "snitch system," where young men are compelled to "tell" on each other in exchange for some type of leniency.

    We need to understand our situation and in order to do that we have to understand the role that manipulation is playing in pitting us against one another. It was Norman Vincent Peale who once wrote, "Understanding can overcome any situation, however mysterious or insurmountable it may appear to be." People who are without power fall prey to the manipulations of the people who have it. One of the ploys used, over the centuries, has been t he reliable "snitch," the "rat fink," the "tipster," the "weasel," the "stool pigeon," the "squealer," the "deep throat," the "nark" and so on. The purpose of this book is to offer understanding and clarity so that we will no longer fall prey to this society's manipulated manifestations of our reality.

    This book deals with American snitches. But I would be derelict if I didn't point out one of the early snitches in history. I am not a Christian and I view the Bible as nothing more than a comic book with some philosophy sprinkled in. But even a broken clock can be right twice a day, and for that reason I am going to give brief mention to one Judas Iscariot.

> There are several explanations as to why Judas betrayed Jesus ,,,
> In the earliest account, in the Gospel of Mark, **when he goes to the chief priests to betray Jesus, he is offered money as a reward, but it is not clear that money is his motivation** … In the Gospel of Matthew account, on the other hand, he asks what they will pay him for handing Jesus over ,,, In the Gospel of Luke ,,, and the Gospel of John … **the devil enters into Judas, causing him to offer to betray Jesus.** The Gospel of John

> account has Judas complaining that money has been spent on expensive perfumes to anoint Jesus which could have been spent on the poor, but adds that he was the keeper of the apostles' purse and used to steal from it (Wikipedia, 2018 – emphasis added)

The motivation is not the point. The point is that Judas sold out Jesus for six pieces of silver. And that six pieces of silver metaphorically exists to this very day and the cops are offering it, the government is offering as is anybody who wants to get someone to betray another person or tell a secret. In this country it is the American way. Black kids are killing each other and a few people blame the snitch system. But they don't put enough emphasis on the historical roots or retroactive abuse of the powers that be in establishing that "confidential informant/snitch" system.

I say, "Give it a name!"

For example, in Omaha the word on the street from these wannabe gang bangers when it came to prison and snitching was "there's two kinds of people; those who told and those who wish they told." This is a long way from the "keep your mouth shut" and "snitches get stitches" that our people used to hold dear. Of course many of the ones saying this were using it as a cover so that they would be above suspicion, but the fact is we knew the danger of "telling." Far too many of our uprisings during enslavement fell short because one of the members of the enslaved class got weak and decided to run and tell the "master."

This book wants to provide some context as well as some food for thought. A person "telling" on another one in order to get him/herself a break of some kind is snitching. But there are different levels of snitches. As you will see in this book, Kobe Bryant snitched on Shaquille O'Neal when he got busted in that rape case in Colorado, claiming "I should have just paid her off like Shaq does his women." This comment ruined Shaq's marriage and Kobe got nothing out of it – he was just a chickenshit muthafucka.

Most of the snitches that are of fame are Italian mob-types. They drop dimes like it's lunch. Once caught they talk and talk and talk. Only a few are mentioned here, but the American white man is quick to make movies about them including "Goodfellas" where snitch Henry Hill served as a consultant to the movie. Other snitches are of a historical type, Benedict Arnold being the most well-known, but there are others that are documented in this book. Elia Kazan was an academy-award winning director and during the "communist scare of the '50s" he told on everybody and Hollywood hated his guts for doing so. And to this very day they have not forgotten what he did.

This list is long and diverse and I want to share this information with my people so these kids will understand that a snitch is not only a personal decision, but a political one. Most of the snitches are not black and in fact, are members of organized crime, manipulated by the FBI as were several black snitches during the 1960s. But we can still learn and in doing so, we can gain "understanding."

Today in black communities all over the country, black kids are shooting and killing each other because of somebody "telling" on them. The cops in these communities instigate and fan these flames of discontent by "dropping dimes" on these kids, spreading the word on who told what, and then standing back while the murders take place.

INTRODUCTION

Three important points that I want to touch upon in order to get to what I consider the "root" of the snitch system in America. As I see it the first issue worthy of discussion is some random history on the subject of betrayal in order to provide context and show that the original snitches (Benedict Arnold is the most famous) in this country. A second point I address is that of the Witness Protection Program and its "reward the snitch" emphasis and orientation. The third issue is that of the police and their use of what they call, "the confidential informant."

A Random List of Traitors and Treachery in U.S. History

Please remember that the following list is simply being provided to show some semblance of scope and context to the art and science of being a sellout, a canary, stoolie, tattletale, a traitor or a snitch. I believe that the names that follow and the betrayals these men have accorded to them clearly show that the street level "snitching" taking place in present-day America are miniscule in terms of scope (not deaths or long-term impact) when compared to the impact that some of the double-crossing that is documented below lays out.

BENEDICT ARNOLD (1780)

We may as well begin with the man whose name is most associated with treachery and that would be General Benedict Arnold. According to once source,

> Benedict Arnold (January 14, 1741 [O.S. January 3, 1740]– June 14, 1801) was an American military officer who **served as a general during the American Revolutionary War, fighting for the American Continental Army before defecting to the British in 1780.** George Washington had **given him his fullest trust and placed him in command of the fortifications at West Point, New York**. Arnold planned to surrender the fort to British forces, but the plot was discovered in September 1780 and he fled to the British. His name quickly became a byword in the United States for treason and betrayal **because he led the British army in battle against the very men whom he had once commanded** (Wikipedia, 2018 – emphasis added)

This is what is so hurtful about snitches and traitors. They win your trust and you confide in them. Today's TV shows clearly show how "tight" some of these men get with the higher ups in an organization and movies do it even better. Classic examples are "Donnie Brasco," the thug Pussy in "The Sopranos, David Kleinfeld of "Carlito's Way," and Whitey Bulger in "Black Mass" to name but a few.

I know Washington, the "Father of this racist country" was truly hurt having trusted Arnold the way he did. It is funny that when Washington's bio is shared with students, rarely is his appointment of Benedict Arnold even mentioned. This was a lapse in leadership on Washington's part; it showed that he made a major mistake and in doing it, he should have been court-martialed and expelled from service. But nope. He lived and today young kids are fed the bullshit myth that "George Washington never told a lie." The fact is, George Washington was as bad as Benedict Arnold because he LIVED a lie.

DENMARK VESEY (1822)

Being a black scholar you know I'm going to include some of the bruthas that were involved in getting snitched on. In the case of Denmark Vesey, we almost had it going on, but got tommed out.

The story is indeed a tragic one:

> **Due to the vast number of slaves who knew about the planned uprising, Vesey feared that word of the plot would get out.** Vesey reportedly advanced the date of the insurrection to June 16.[17] Beginning in May, two slaves opposed to Vesey's scheme, George Wilson and Joe LaRoche, gave the first specific

> testimony about a coming uprising to Charleston officials, saying a "rising" was planned for July 14. George Wilson was a mixed-race slave who was deeply loyal to his master. (Wikipedia, 2018 – emphasis added).

That first sentence gave it away to me, and is a key to learning about the snitch system. The more people who know, the more likely you are to be betrayed. I learned a long time ago not to tell the woman in your life anything you want to remain a secret. First of all, most relationships don't last or at least they don't remain rockstrong. Since that is the case the one who you "trusted" will lose her value and loyalty over time.

But more importantly than that, anything you tell a woman you can be sure of one thing: at least one other bitch knows. Women talk to each other and that means that whatever you share with your woman, no matter how intimate, she is going to share with her "girlfriend."

What does that have to do with Denmark Vesey? How are you going to plan a revolt that is still in its infancy and tell every asshole on the plantation about it? The "mixed race" issue is one that I deal with under a separate cover but trust me: if you're half white, then you're only half "alright" in my book. Those people have mixed loyalties from birth, and I know some good bruthas and sistahs who are of mixed race. But I also know that people tend to love their mothers and that white mother is going to be the "exception" to any rule that exists. These black people are not going to say or mean anything negative about "dear ol' mama."

So the mixed race brutha probably wanted to curry favor with his master. If he snitches, he will win some brownie points. That is the reward system at work and that is what is at work with these young snitches today when they tell what they know in exchange for leniency in prison sentences, arrests on the streets and so on.

In the case of Vesey,

> **The testimonies of these two men confirmed an earlier report coming from another slave named Peter Prioleau.** Though officials didn't believe the less specific testimony of Prioleau, they did believe Wilson and LaRoche **due to their unimpeachable reputations with their masters.** With their testimony, the city launched **a search for conspirators** (Wikipedia, 2018 – emphasis added)

There is a hierarchy even in the snitch system. The white man has some sellouts that he trusts more than others. In this case the white man had a backup set of "canaries" that had already snitched and all he needed was verification because no matter how much the white man trusts a black person, that racial hate still creates a shield of traditional fear and that leads to some skepticism.

The psychology of the snitch is also quite evident, as we can glean from the following excerpt:

> Joe LaRoche had originally planned to support the rising and brought the slave Rolla Bennett to discuss plans with George Wilson, his close friend. **Wilson had to decide whether to join the conspiracy described by Bennett or tell his master that there was a plot in the making.** Wilson refused to join the conspiracy and urged both Laroche and Bennett to end their involvement in the plans. **Wilson convinced LaRoche that they must tell his master to prevent the conspiracy from being acted out** (Wikipedia, 2018 – emphasis added)

When the group of two (a "dyad") becomes the group of three (a "triad") power shifts begin to take place somewhere in the group. In this case, LaRouche evidently had some hidden "trust" in Wilson and wanted a fellow "slave" to come and meet him. Wilson was indecisive but managed to get the other two to side with him because he probably sensed that they didn't really want to go through with it either.

And so the snitches informed on Vesey and his crew:

> The Mayor James Hamilton was told, and he organized a citizens' militia, **putting the city on alert.** White militias and groups of armed men patrolled the streets daily for weeks until **many suspects were arrested by the end of June, including 55-year-old Denmark Vesey** … As suspects were arrested, they were held in the Charleston Workhouse until the **newly appointed Court of Magistrates and Freeholders heard evidence against them.** (Wikipedia, 2018 – emphasis added)

As you can see the process of suppression became ritualized. The white man gives chase, captures the people that were snitched on, locks them up and then in a public spectacle places the snitches in front of those who got told on. This kind of degradation ceremony takes place to this very day but today there is a new twist: the addition of the "witness protection program."

And the story comes to an end:

> **The Workhouse was also the place where punishment was applied to slaves for their masters, and likely where Plot**

> **suspects were abused or threatened with abuse or death before giving testimony to the Court** … The suspects were allowed visits by ministers; Dr. Benjamin Palmer visited Vesey when he was sentenced to death, and Vesey told the minister that he would die for a "glorious cause" (Wikipedia, 2018 – emphasis added)

At no time in this "law and order" environment do these peckerwoods question the moral legitimacy of the "master-slave relationship." That is a given for the most part. So they tiptoe around that reality and turn the victim of this major social atrocity into the culprit who "dared" to try to escape from being enslaved.

ANNA SAGE (1934) - Dillinger's Deadly Date

This woman was "used" by the FBI so they could finally get their hands on John Dillinger. She was an informant of the worst kind: a female who gained the trust of a wanted criminal so that she could escape being deported from this country.

As one source explains it,

> Anna Sage was a **Romanian immigrant** who came to America in 1909 and found work in a brothel in East Chicago, Ind. Although she was successful in this venerable and established field (she opened several of her own houses of ill repute in Indiana and Illinois), the Department of Labor sought to deport her as an "alien of low moral character."• But when famed bank robber John Dillinger—whom she met through mutual gal pal Polly Hamilton—asked her to a movie, Sage thought she'd **found a way to stamp her Green Card**. Dillinger was wanted in five states, and Sage hoped that if she turned him in, the good karma would translate into an invitation to stay in the U.S. (Mental Floss, 2008 – emphasis added)

So this "snitch" was given a deal – turn on Dillinger and set him up and she would get her green card. Ain't that a bitch? There was no way that the government was going to take Dillinger alive, and that is a fact. He made them look stupid on numerous occasions and made fun of them. The FBI took it personally. And they used this woman to help get Dillinger out in the open where they could "legally" assassinate him.

Now, the details:

> To stage the arrest, Sage called her ex-boyfriend, Martin Zarkovich, at the East Chicago Police Department, and was put in contact with agent Melvin Purvis, who was working the Dillinger case for the FBI. **Sage told Purvis about her upcoming date with Dillinger at the Biograph Theater on July 22, 1934. (O.k., maybe she didn't specify the year"!)** In order to be identified in the crowd, **Sage agreed to wear a white blouse and orange skirt that night, even though history would later dub her the "Lady in Red."**• (Historians believe the lights of the marquee made her outfit appear red, spawning the moniker.) As she, Dillinger, and Polly Hamilton exited the theater, Purvis confronted the group. **Dillinger tried to run, which worked pretty well until four FBI bullets put a hitch in his stride. He died at the scene.** (Mental Floss, 2008 – emphasis added)

You just read what took place. It was a setup from the very start. A "deal" was cut which is vital in order for a "snitch" to earn his/her stripes.

ELIA KAZAN (1950s)

It seems as if the white immigrants – mainly the Jews, Italians and Irish – have a tendency to snitch on one another when times get tight. The same can now be said of black people too, although it was not always the case. Incidents like Denmark Vesey and others were the exception, not the rule. But this case of Elia Kazan (who was Greek) is about those Hollywood Jews and the "communist scare" of the 1950s.

According to a website called Mental Floss,

> **Between 1945 and 1957, Elia Kazan enjoyed a hot streak few in Hollywood could even dream about.** He directed 13 acclaimed motion pictures (including "A Streetcar Named Desire"• and "East of Eden"•) and **was nominated for four Best Director awards.** Kazan was riding high when Hollywood entered the **blackest period** in its history (barring the second and third installments of the "Matrix"• trilogy): the Communist witch hunts of the 1950's. (Mental Floss, 2015 – emphasis added)

Again, the impact of white imagery is pervasive as the period that is the most negative is described as being "the blackest." This is white supremacy at work, as was the entire existence of Hollywood, founded and created by Jews who were too cheap to keep paying Thomas Edison for the rights to materials needed to make film, so what did they do? They went over to Europe and "replicated" the process, made their own film materials and then came back to America. And since Edison was doing his work on the east coast, the Jews set up shop on the west coast and voila! Hollywood was born.

And from its inception it was white nationalism pure and simple. The movies promoted the American way of life, glorified white women, painted white men as virile and powerful and poked fun at blacks, Mexicans, First Nation people and Asians. No movie then or now can be made without being approved (referred to as being "green lighted") without the approval of some Jewish person. They hide this fact and are embarrassed when it's mentioned. To talk or write about it is immediately deemed "anti-Semitic."

Their fear of being exposed is what made so many of them turn on each other during the period known as the "Communist scare" or the "Hollywood blacklist." Again, just as the writer of the snippet refers to a negative period as "the blackest," any list that contains negative information is dubbed a "Blacklist." Racism permeates America throughout all spheres. As one source explains it,

> The Hollywood blacklist – as the broader entertainment industry blacklist is generally known – **was the practice of denying employment to screenwriters, actors, directors, musicians, and American entertainment professionals during the mid-20th century** because they were accused of having Communist ties or sympathies. Artists were barred from work on the basis of their membership, alleged membership in, or sympathy with the Communist Party USA**, or their refusal to assist investigations into the party's activities.** (Wikipedia, 2018)

As it relates to Kazan, specifically, he was a Greek but had the same fear and concern for his profession as every other white ethnic did. Another source outlines how he turned "snitch":

> A philosophical and politically passionate man, **Kazan had been a founding member of the leftist Group Theater in New York and, for a little more than a year, was a member of the Communist Party.** In 1934, however, Kazan's ideals began to diverge sharply from those of the Party, and he soon **found himself a zealous anti-Communist.** Wanting names, the government pressured Kazan to spill the beans, even threatening to have him **blacklisted by major Hollywood studios**. (Mental Floss, 2015 – emphasis added)

Threats from the government, a key approach to use when wanting to "flip" someone and get them to become an informant. Remember the case of

Anna Savage when the FBI wanted to "get" John Dillinger some sixteen years earlier? The snitch system was still in effect and was the same thing in this case. Kazan wanted to direct and continue making a living and he had to snitch in order to continue to do it.

The got him to "turn":

> After wrestling with the question of whether or not he should sacrifice his career for people whose ideals he disdained, **Kazan decided to share his knowledge of Communists in Hollywood with the House Committee on Un-American Activities**. In 1952, he went before the Committee and **named eight of his Group Theater buddies who had been members of the Communist Party with him.** (Mental Floss, 2015 – emphasis added)

He turned on people who had at one time been his friends. This is the decision that a number of snitches have to make. The threats of the government can get people to turn on those they have slept with or been married to. Sometimes it's the threat of getting locked up and other times it's the offer of money and a new identity (which I deal with later in this book). At any rate, America is no "peaches and cream" nation that operates above board. Don't forget how they killed members of the Black Panther Party back in the 1960s with the full approval of the government and its leadership.

The Kazan case continues:

> After Kazan's testimony, **the government was fast on the tails of those he'd named,** pressuring them for **yet more names**, and it was officially witchhuntin' season! **Many actors, writers, and directors were blacklisted,** and scores of careers were ruined. The era remains one of the least tinselly in Tinseltown history. (Mental Floss, 2015 – emphasis added)

The nickname "Tinseltown" refers to the glitz and glamour of a place that grew far beyond just a movie lot or two. According to a Hollywood.com website,

> By 1915, America was officially film crazed, and Hollywood was shaping into the glamorous, sometimes surreal landscape we've come to know and love. Hopeful actors and actresses filled the streets, dazzled by a new American dream: film stardom. Studios, meanwhile, sprung up like wildfires and engaged in a cutthroat battle for survival. As the industry matured, many of these

independent companies merged, forming the big studios that would shape and control the industry moving forward. By 1920, 40 million Americans were going to the movies each week (Hollywoodsign.org, 2015)

Kazan became the bane of Hollywood for his snitching:

> Not surprisingly, pretty much everyone not already in the business of rooting out Commies reviled Kazan. His longtime friend and confidant, Arthur Miller, explained his feelings on the matter in his allegorical play "The Crucible."• **Not to be outdone, Kazan shot back by crafting a sympathetic informer character in his film "On The Waterfront,"**• **which Miller rebutted in "A View From The Bridge"** (Mental Floss, 2015 = emphasis added)

So when you watch "Straight Outta Compton" and watch the rap wars go back and forth and Ice Cube getting payback with "No Vaseline," you have to realize that Jews have been playing these games long before these black rappers were even born. You just read an example of it. Once you snitch, people don't forget it:

> But the controversy surrounding Kazan was yet to abate. **In 1999, Kazan was presented with a lifetime achievement award at the Oscars, and more than 500 people showed up to protest.** Writer and director Abraham Polonsky, whom 20th Century Fox had fired and blacklisted for his refusal to cooperate with the House Un-American Activities Committee, said of the event, **"I'll be watching, hoping someone shoots him** (Mental Floss, 2008 – emphasis added)

And there you have the threat of death in response to someone snitching – just like you find on the streets of the ghetto today. No one, black or white, likes a snitch. But America continues to promote it as some type of "noble act" and local TV stations offer programs like "WeTip" pledging to pay the poor for information that leads not only to an arrest, but an actual *conviction*.

WALT DISNEY (1950s)

I want to say here and now that no matter what the apologists or revisionist historians say, I say that Disney was a racist. The existing cartoons and even movies that he made backin the '50s on until today, smack of racism and ethnic bias.

Some background information is necessary:

> **Disney has been accused of anti-Semitism ... although none of his employees—including the animator Art Babbitt, who disliked Disney intensely—ever accused him of making anti-Semitic slurs or taunts ...** The Walt Disney Family Museum acknowledges that ethnic stereotypes common to films of the 1930s were included in some early cartoons ... Disney donated regularly to Jewish charities, **he was named "1955 Man of the Year" by the B'nai B'rith chapter in Beverly Hills** ... and his **studio employed a number of Jews, some of whom were in influential positions** (Wikipedia, 2018 – emphasis added)

The previous excerpt is so typical of the apologists and their shallow attempts at an explanation, on-going ways to defuse or deflect the racism of celebrities, especially Jews. I am going to deal with these deflections point-by-point to show how this is done and to clearly demonstrate the abysmal ignorance of those who claim to know history and yet spend most of their time falling prey to it.

To begin with, the claim that none of Disney's employees ever accused him of making "anti-Semitic slurs or taunts." That doesn't mean a damn thing. Black employees are discriminated against every day of the year and many have never heard a white man or woman come close to uttering the word "nigger" a single time. And do you know why? Because first of all these racists know the law and are very careful. Secondly there is no need to use racial slurs or taunts when every day at that job you treat "those people" the way that you believe they need to be treated. The statement about anti-Semitic slurs is therefore ludicrous.

Secondly, Disney being named "Man of the Year" in 1955 by the major Jewish organization, B'nai B'rith. Again, so what? Disney was powerful and employed a large number of Jews. Jews know this so they therefore cater to the employer. They kiss his ass and give him an award in the same way that the NAACP gives white racists awards because those racists make sizable donations. Disney knew he was no "Man of the Year.' Man of the Year for what? For doing what? Playing with cartoons? Promoting racist stereotypes in film and on television?

Third, the claim that Disney studios employed a number of Jews and that some of them were "in influential position." This brings us back to the reason for number two. Of course Jews had influence in Disney studios because Disney was the "outsider" who had posted up in a Jewish stronghold known as Hollywood. He hired Jews in the same way that the white managers and presidents of clothing stores post up in the ghetto and then hire black men and women to serve as high visibility "managers" of those stores.

Revisionist history protects Disney the same way that it protects other white racists over the years:

> Gabler, the first writer to gain unrestricted access to the Disney archives, **concludes that the available evidence does not support accusations of anti-Semitism and that Disney was "not [anti-Semitic] in the conventional sense that we think of someone as being an anti-Semite"**. Gabler concludes that "though Walt himself, in my estimation, was not anti-Semitic, nevertheless, he willingly allied himself with people who were anti-Semitic and that reputation stuck. He was never really able to expunge it throughout his life"(Wikipedia, 2018 – emphasis added)

So what? What did Gabler expect to find – a giant poster with the statement, "I hate Hymies"? A sign that reads "Kill the Kikes"? If you ally yourself with people who are racist, you are a racist if you're laughing at their jokes and not doing anything to keep them from insulting and harming black people.

Revisionist can compile reams of "evidence" that Disney wasn't anti-Semitic or racist, but that is the purpose of revisionists. Disney was no more than the context to which he owed his existence. Therefore it was impossible to work in Hollywood and be white and not be racist, either consciously or unconsciously.

Back to the snitch allegations.

It was the 1950s and the Jews were running Hollywood, just as they do now. And when the government began cracking down on communism, a lot of them sold each other out and spilled their guts. Unbeknownst to a lot of people, Walt Disney had been a long time "informant" for the FBI:

> There are almost as many myths and half truths about Walt Disney as there are people in line for Space Mountain on any given weekend: his frozen body is kept below Disney Land, he was a Nazi sympathizer (probably true), he was an FBI Informant, the list goes on.(Shelton, 2015)

If it was "probably true" that he was a Nazi sympathizer, then it was also equally true that he was a racist. If he was a racist then he must have also been anti-Semitic because Nazis hated the Jews. And if he was anti-Semitic and anti-Black, then he was the perfect person to work for the FBI because J. Edgar Hoover and his "bureau" were both anti-Semitic and anti-Black – as history bears out. Now you can see why I prefaced this section with background on Disney and the context that he worked in.

According to Shelton,

> According to documents obtained under the Freedom of Information Act, **it seems that Walt Disney served as a secret FBI informant for 26 years** and allowed J. Edgar Hoover access to movie and TV scripts **so the agency director could suggest changes.** Maybe that's why there's so much cross dressing in all those early Disney films. (Shelton, 2015 – emphasis added)

Shelton attempts to be joking about the cross-dressing but the reality would be that if J. Edgar Hoover had gleaned any movies he would have probably suggested the elimination of anything hinting at cross dressing because it was what he believed in. But he need not have worried: the effeminate Jews of Hollywood were way ahead of him. They were dressing men up as women long before Hoover was even born. It seems to be a part of the white male's value system to do so. Ask Dave Chapelle.

RONALD REAGAN

Again, we go back to Hollywood and a famous name comes to the fore. Ronald Reagan, who would go on to become President of the United States in the 1980s, was a former informant for the FBI. A "snitch."

> Before he was the 40th president of the United States, Ronald Reagan lived out his days in Hollyweird, acting in films like *Bedtime for Bonzo* and *Hellcats of the Navy*. This is common knowledge. But did you know that as a budding politician in Hollywood's acting community after World War II, **Reagan served as a confidential informant for the FBI, snitching about pro-Communist influences in the Screen Actors Guild and other Hollywood organizations?** (Shelton, 2015 – emphasis added)

Whether it's the fear of organized crime, of Communism or later on, a fear of a black revolutionary takeover, these white people have developed a system where the "confidential informant" enables them to destroy most forms of resistance to their system.

MICHAEL FORTIER (1997)

Remember the Oklahoma City bombing? How do you think the FBI caught Timothy McVeigh, who had all but gotten away with it? A snitch, that's how:

> Michael and Lori Fortier were considered accomplices for their foreknowledge of the planning of the Oklahoma City bombing in 1995. Among their activities, Michael assisted McVeigh in scouting the federal building and Lori had helped McVeigh laminate a fake driver's license which was later used to rent the Ryder truck used to deliver the explosives. (Shelton, 2015).

So this set of snitches were a part of the operation and the FBI got them to "flip" on McVeigh who, up until that time, seemed to have committed the perfect crime. For a country that was born in revolutionary action against England, these white people are sure afraid of any act that shows any sign of rebellion against THEIR tyranny, from Denmark Vesey and Benedict Arnold and here we are now in the 1990s and they are still sowing discord in the ranks of those they fear and getting prospective dissidents to "spill the beans" on each other.

Continuing:

> **Michael agreed to testify against McVeigh and Nichols in exchange for a reduced sentence and immunity for his wife**. On May 27, 1998, he was sentenced to 12 years in prison and fined $75,000 for failing to warn authorities about the attack. On January 20, 2006, after serving ten and a half years of his sentence, including time already served, **Fortier was released for good behavior into the Witness Protection Program and given a new identity.** (Shelton, 2015 – emphasis added)

And so another revolutionary act is quashed because of a snitch. McVeigh was a piece of shit, but he had the right idea about America and that it needed to be taught a lesson. I'm not sure if those children inside of the building he blew up deserved what they got, but then that is the price of being a part of an oppressive system. Sometimes the little ones have to pay, too.

LEROY "NICKI" BARNES

Today's naïve millennial sissies don't know their history and when the movie "American Gangster" came out, they saw Nicki Barnes, the rival of main gangster and drug dealer Frank Lucas, and they thought he was the greatest. But was he? According to the research,

> Leroy "Nicky" Barnes, aka "Mr. Untouchable," was one of the biggest drug lords in American history and leader of The Council, an African-American gang in the 1970s. When he was arrested and sentenced to life in prison, he discovered The Council had stopped paying his attorneys' fees, **and one of his fellow council members, Guy Fisher, was having an affair with his mistress. As a result, he turned over 109 names, including that of his wife, and helped convict 16 criminals.** (Shelton, 2015 - emphasis added)

I'm not so sure that Barnes snitched based on the order of the reasons given above. I think he heard that somebody was tapping his woman and that is what sent him off the deep end. But whatever the reason was, the turned snitch. TVOne ran a piece called, "Top 5 Notorious Gangsters Turned Informants," and here's what they had to say about Barnes:

> Leroy "Nicky" Barnes is yet another legendary Harlem drug dealer. During the 1970s, Barnes would control the Heroin trade in Harlem. Barnes would wear a lot of flashy clothes and drive expensive cars setting a precedent for other Harlem drug dealers to follow. After appearing on the New York Times Magazine cover with a fur coat on, he drew the attention of President Jimmy Carter, who ordered the Attorney General to prosecute him to the fullest extent of the law. After being convicted and sentenced to jail, **Barnes would learn that some of his associates were sleeping with some of his women.** Barnes ended up testifying against 44 of his former cohorts, which led to the convictions of 16 of them including legendary drug dealer, Guy Fischer.(Cganemccalla, 2011)

Conspicuous consumption will get you every time. At least Tim McVeigh had the brains to go underground. But people like Dillinger and Barnes – they can't help themselves. Even today with these young punks that I write about later, you can find them on Facebook posing with tens of thousands of dollars in cash, lying across the bed swimming in it, standing next to high-end automobiles and then the cops come. After they get tuned up and spend a little time behind bars, they turn snitch so that they can once again smell the sweet air of freedom – or at least the American version of it.

Snitches and confidential informants realize what they've done only after they've done it. Like the kids in Omaha were saying back in the summer about a decade back, "There's those who told and those who wish they'd told."

JOSE CANSECO

Canseco was a hero in Oakland and he was knocking the ball out of the park on the field and with the women. But then he got stupid and wrote a book and TOLD on a whole bunch of fellow players, all of whom were using steroids.

> Jose Canseco might be one of the best baseball players ever, but that doesn't change the fact that he snitched on a whole bunch of fellow steroid-loving MLB players. In his hit tell-all book, *Juiced: Wild Times, Rampant 'Roids, Smash Hits & How Baseball Got Big* he named former teammates including Mark McGwuire, Jorge Delgado, Damaso Moreno, and Manuel Collado. (Shelton, 2015)

But it was much deeper than what was just described because Canseco did not just write about what others did. He provided vivid detail, cracked jokes and basically made fun of them in the process. Here is some background research to show all the money he made, all the exposure he got and finally, as is the case with many "informants," his regrets that he ever "told."

When the book was initially published, Canseco made an appearance on CBS News on February 10, 2005. Following are his comments regarding and my analysis of what took place.

> Jose Canseco, variously called "The Bad Boy of Baseball," or "The Godfather of Steroids," has written a much-talked-about book he calls "Juiced" that purports to tell the truth about his own use of anabolic steroids and human growth hormones, and the same about other top players in Major League Baseball. The book is already a best-seller, due to pre-orders on Amazon and elsewhere. Yet almost no one has read it, because it won't be available until Monday morning. (Hancock, 2005)

So Canseco made money for "telling" on others. He injected steroids which in turn, gave him super powers and he set all kinds of records and gained fame from it. Then, for some reason, after injecting some of his pals as well, he decided he could make money if he just "spilled the beans" and informed the public about what he had done. And like many (if not most) snitches, he was rewarded for his betrayal.

Continuing:

> In the book and in this broadcast, **Canseco names names** - some of them superstar players - all of whom have categorically denied his charges. But none of them agreed to talk to *60 Minutes* on camera about it, though they and many others are publicly calling Canseco nasty names, mainly a liar. (Hancock, 2005)

> But Canseco tells **Correspondent Mike Wallace**, in his first interview discussing his controversial book, that he's prepared for that. **"Baseball is the national pastime, and what you're saying is that the national past time is juiced," Wallace asks Canseco. "Yeah. It is. And it's reality," says Canseco**. Is he now taking on the whole baseball establishment? "I don't know if I'm directly trying to take on the whole baseball establishment," says Canseco. "I'm just basically telling a story of my life." (Hancock, 2005 – emphasis added)

This form of snitching is somewhat different because Canseco told on his associates strictly for money. He wasn't in any kind of trouble. He just did it. In a way, this might be the worst kind of snitch, a kind of "voluntary provocateur." Furthermore,

> His book, "Juiced," has put Major League Baseball and its author on the hot seat. **Canseco writes about his 16-year career as a Major League ball player, and he says that from his first season, to his last in 2001, he used illegal anabolic steroids and human growth hormones."** You essentially strengthened your body and your performance with a cocktail of steroids and growth hormones," says Wallace."Yes," says Canseco. Where did he inject it? **"Into your gluteus maximus, which is your butt muscle," says Canseco, who admits it's illegal to use, unless prescribed and administered by a licensed doctor**. (Hancock, 2005 – emphasis added)

Writing about his career and his use of steroids is one thing. But what makes him a snitch, a sellout and a provocateur is that he starts naming other people, knowing full well that those people are going to catch as much hell as he did. He is jeopardizing their families and careers just like any snitch does to the people that he tells on. These types of tattlers just don't care; all they want is what they are after which is usually protection, money or some kind of reward or payment.

The fact is that Canseco benefited from the use of those drugs:

> Those illegal drugs helped fuel a larger-than-life career for Canseco, whose many home runs were monster shots. In 1988, Canseco hit 42 home runs and stole 40 bases. It was a feat never seen before. "You say this, 'I would never have been a Major League-caliber player without steroids.' Right," asks Wallace. "Well, it's a true statement. No ifs and buts about it," says Canseco. (Hancock, 2005) And how much of his career success does he attribute to the use of steroids?"Maybe not accomplish the things I did, the freakish things I did, being 6'4", 250, running 4-340's, the 40-40. Hitting 600-foot home runs. Who knows," says Canseco. "A lot of it is psychological. I mean, you really believe you have an edge. You feel the strength, and the stamina." (Hancock, 2005)

Canseco took drugs and became a legend. Even if he didn't get away with it, the writing of the book would have made him financially secure for the rest of his life. But what makes him a snitch is that he told on others, and the question is why would he do that? He did it because a key part of the personality and character of the sellout is to please the master. If he tells on pro baseball players he can appear to be "above board." But he went even further than that:

> "What you're saying is that you were a living steroids experiment for your entire career," says Wallace."Yes, that's what I was," says Canseco, who claims he knows more about steroids than most trained physicians, and that he actively counseled other players about using anabolic steroids and human growth hormone. (Hancock, 2005)

In another article Canseco says he wrote the book as a form of "payback":

> During the program, the 44-year-old **Canseco said he "wanted revenge" on Major League Baseball because he believed he had been forced out of the game. The book was his means of getting even, and he named names** "to show I was telling the truth" about steroids in baseball, he said.Canseco last played in 2001 and retired in 2002 with 462 career home runs, a .266 batting average, 1,407 RBIs and 200 stolen bases for eight major league clubs. (ESPN.com, 2008 – emphasis added)

Canseco has regrets for snitching. The headline of an October 21, 2008 article in ESPN.com says it all: "Canseco regrets naming names in his book about steroids."

> Jose Canseco, whose book "Juiced," which focused attention on the use of performance-enhancing drugs in Major League Baseball and led to congressional hearings on the subject, now says he never should have written the book and named names of alleged steroid users. During the A&E Network's one-hour documentary, "Jose Canseco: The Last Shot," Canseco said he "regrets mentioning players [as steroid users]. I never realized this was going to blow up and hurt so many people." (ESPN.com, 2008)

Canseco may be telling the truth when he says that he had no idea how many people he would be hurting. The snitch, the rat, the tattler doesn't give a shit about who gets hurt. He's concerned about his own well being. But one thing that Canseco knew is that the people that he NAMED would be hurt, and that is what makes a snitch a snitch. They get the money because they name the people, no matter who the people are.

And he says that the Commissioner at the time Bud Selig, knew about the "juicing" and just turned a blind eye. This is the kind of behavior that sells more books, leads to more national appearances in person and on television, and makes you the kind of celebrity that you are seeking to be.

It's also the kind of behavior that makes you a "snitch."

LINDA TRIPP (1998)

Like many others, she knew she was going to snitch from the get-go. She befriended a white girl who was even more weak-minded that she was and got her to spill the beans on her affair with the President of the United States. As the Time committee writer explained it:

> In what has now become a tired punch line, Linda Tripp was a key figure in the Clinton/Lewinski scandal that took over American news in the mid '90s. **Tripp was a confidant of Monica Lewinski and surreptitiously recorded the conversations, acting on the advice of literary agent Luciana Goldberg.** Based on **Tripp's tapes, a federal case was built around Lewinski's alleged perjury and the Clinton/Lewinski scandal hit critical mass.** (Shelton, 2015 – emphasis added)

That young girl trusted Tripp, which is a key to any good snitch: win the trust of the person or people that you are going to tell on. Once a person trusts you, they will say anything and/or answer any questions that you pose to them. And Tripp didn't just tell on Lewinsky and Clinton: she spilled the beans on the system and its perversely parasitic sexual trysts, in general:

> The woman who exposed former President Bill Clinton's affair with Monica Lewinsky said the president had "thousands" of similar affairs and if she hadn't spoken out when she did, she and Lewinsky would both likely be dead. **Linda Tripp**, a former friend of Lewinsky who worked at the White House during the same time as the infamous intern, said in a radio interview Sunday with Aaron Klein that she believed her and Lewinsky's lives were in imminent danger. (Sabia, 2016)

Now that she's dropped a dime she wants to come off as some kind of super hero. But if you saw a photo of Linda Tripp it would be apparent that she needed friends. She was the fat unattractive girl that went out of her way to be nice so people wouldn't make fun of her. She dyed her hair blond (I suppose it was dye) so she could fit in. Then she meets an equally weak-minded, younger white woman and befriends her.

After the news broke the word got out and "snitch" was all you heard. She became the butt of TV jokes, even worse than poor Monica. But Tripp went on the defensive in an attempt to salvage some modicum of dignity out of the situation:

> "I say today and I will continue to say that I believe **Monica Lewinsky** is alive today because of choices I made and action I took," she said. "That may sound melodramatic to your listeners. I can only say that from my perspective **I believe that she and I at the time were in danger, because nothing stands in the way of these people achieving their political ends**," Tripp continues. "Had it not become public when it did… We may well have met with an accident. It's a situation where unless you lived it as I did you would have no real framework of reference for this sort of situation." (Sabia, 2016 – emphasis added)

What Tripp described was the reality of the situation even BEFORE the Lewinsky-Clinton incident. This was nothing new. What was new was that Lewinsky was stupid enough to share what she had done with this older woman. How is that done? What do you say, "Hey guess what? I sucked

President Clinton's dick last night! This makes the fourth time!" How do you brag about something like that?

Clinton got away relatively unscathed. According to Tripp,

> **Tripp said Clinton had affairs with "thousands" of women, including another White House staffer who she declined to name,** and added that it was "common knowledge," even to Mrs. Hillary Clinton, whose involvement in the scandal was solely to defame and discredit the women involved. "She made it her personal mission to disseminate information and destroy the women with whom he dallied," Tripp told Klein. She said that while the former first lady showcases herself as "a champion of women's rights worldwide in a global fashion, and yet **all of the women she has destroyed over the years to ensure her political viability continues is sickening to me."**
> (Sabia, 2016 – emphasis added)

What Tripp says about Hillary Clinton doesn't surprise me. I knew she was a two faced bitch when, during every election campaign, she starts talking about her background working with the poor and the needy and how she went into the neighborhoods and all that shit. While her husband was going after every black woman that moved (and even fathered a child with one), she was acting as if she was some type of feminist. But Tripp knew all this and this is the key to a snitch: they don't tell EVERYTHING they know, just the stuff that will get them paid.

Trip was unattractive and fat and lumbering around Washington, DC looking for a friend. She found on in an under-aged white girl named Monica Lewinski, and won her trust. And when she found out that Monica had sucked Clinton's dick, that is all she needed to get the attention that she had always craved. But she had to fix it so that she (Tripp) could come out looking like a hero because after the initial disclosures people were calling her a backstabber and a snitch.

As the story goes,

> Tripp told Klein that she couldn't stand seeing the American people being duped by the president and Hillary and their lying ways. "All of the scandals that had come before and were so completely obliterated in the mind's eye of the American people because of the way all of them were essentially discounted," she said. **"So my dismay predated the January 1998 period when the Monica Lewinsky scandal surfaced. To me it was very important that the American people see what I was**

seeing. My years with the Clintons were so disturbing on so many levels." (Sabia, 2016)

This is what "white privilege" can do for you: it can buy you time. You can pick and choose your options and your opportunities. You can time things just right so that you come out looking like a hero instead of a zero. And that is what Linda Tripp, the snitch who exposed young Monica Lewinski, came out looking like.

Two points about this snitch and what she did in this historical controversy involving the President of the United States. First, she is 24 years older than Lewinski and used that to her advantage, which brings us to a second point. It was Tripp who told the lawyer Kenneth Starr about the navy blue dress that Lewinsky owned that had Clinton's sperm on it. According to one source, "During their friendship, Lewinsky had shown the dress to Tripp and said she intended to have it dry-cleaned; Tripp convinced her not to" (Wikipedia, 2018).

White privilege protects a lot of these snitches. They seem to always survive the storm. According to a recent article that appeared in the Washington Times under the headline, "Vindication for a Whistleblower," Tripp came out looking as clean and superhero-like as can be:

> Ms. Tripp withdrew to a private life after the scandal, and now she comes in from the cold to reappear on a changed landscape littered with the likes of Harvey Weinstein, Matt Lauer, Kevin Spacey and Charlie Rose. She suggests that the former president, Bill Clinton, should take his place on the pedestal of predators, up there with current celebrities of stage, screen and politics. **"When the president gets a pass for something that egregious,"** she tells the London Daily Mail, **"he essentially gave tacit permission to all those who followed to do the same."** (Fields, 2018 – emphasis added)

Another advantage for the successful snitch is that once the pain that they have caused has been alleviated, they can then use their new found infamy to "revise" historical reality. That is what you just read. This bitch wants the world to think that her snitching is what opened up the eyes of the American public to what these Presidents and other powerful white men were getting away with. The fact is, these white boys have been sexually harassing and assaulting women, girls and little boys since the inception of this country. And they continue to do it and get away with it. And they're doing it in the halls of politics and even around the Catholic church.

SAMMY "THE BULL" GRAVANO: Blabbing on the Boss (1991)

A key to the greatness of the mob and its success is that they have a code of silence known as "omerta." According to one source, the Omerta code of silence is "He who is deaf, blind and silent will live a hundred years in peace." The same source provides even more detail:

> "Omertà is an extreme form of loyalty and solidarity in the face of authority. One of its absolute tenets is that it is deeply demeaning and shameful to betray even one's deadliest enemy to the authorities," writes an Italian author. A mafia member will therefore not call the police when he is a victim of a crime. **A wronged person is expected to solve the problem conclusively on his own**. (Smassaro, 2018 – emphasis added)

I shared all this to pave the way and provide context for establishing the significance of the snitching that Sammy "The Bull" Gravano committed against his Mafia brothers. Once source describes what he did, thusly:

> **Probably the world's most notorious hairdresser-turned-hitman, Salvatore "Sammy The Bull" Gravano was the highest-ranking Italian Mafia member ever to break omerta, the mob code of silence.** Born in Brooklyn and nicknamed "The Bull" for his short stature, thick neck, and ruthless fighting tactics, Gravano rose to the position of underboss in the Gambino crime family. Allegedly responsible for 19 murders, Gravano was no angel, and no tight-lips, either. **Sammy's damning testimony sealed the fate of many in the organization, including his former boss, John Gotti.** (Mental Floss, 2015 – emphasis added)

Gravano was the one who helped bring down John Gotti. After all the dirt he did he was worried about going to prison and what would happen to him. So he dropped a dime the same way a lot of these young black guys do today when the white man surrounds them and intimidates them with tales of being raped and "going away".

But just like Linda Tripp and Jose Canseco, the snitches have a "hero's tale" to tell after they drop that dime and have to face a little public acrimony. For instance,

> The reason Gravano snitched varies depending on whom you ask. Some claim **he did it to receive a lighter prison sentence**, while

others say **he got mad after hearing Gotti badmouthing him on a wiretap.** But in Underboss: Sammy The Bull Gravano's Life In The Mafia, **Gravano says Gotti needed to be taken down because he was addicted to publicity, and all the attention was harming the mob.** Either way, Gravano delivered such damaging testimony in court that lead Gotti prosecutor John Gleeson described him as having **rendered "extraordinary, unprecedented, historic assistance to the government."** (Mental Floss, 2008 – emphasis added)

How would he have heard about Gotti badmouthing him on a wiretap unless he was already snitching or considering it? You could easily label this tough guy, this big time gangster as a "super snitch" because what he told the government about his former pals nearly crippled the organization, as the following excerpt explains:

Information provided by Gravano created a ripple effect throughout the Mafia underground, and numerous corroborating witnesses came forward. Dozens of luminaries in the Cosa Nostra crime syndicate were convicted, jury-rigging schemes were exposed, mobsters already in jail had their sentences extended, **and high-ranking members of the Gambino, Colombo, DeCalvacante, and Lucchese families were imprisoned.** In 1995, Gravano got a cushy five-year sentence for his 19 murders, and was later placed in the **Witness Protection Program.** After his release, Sammy made the most of his second chance by **teaming up with some neo-Nazis and getting busted for selling Ecstasy ...** He got 19 years in the slammer this time, a sentence he's still serving. (Mental Floss, 2008 – emphasis added)

Snitching bred more snitching and the walls came tumbling down. Gravano got away with it and everything was fine. But as you just read he couldn't stay away from the criminal life and ended up going back to prison. But that's not the point being made here. The point is that he went back to prison for selling Ecstasy and got nineteen years. That's a year for every life he took before he ratted out the crime families. For those crimes he only got five years. The system places mob activity and imprisonment far above doing the right thing. But they don't do a damn thing about dealing ecstasy.

KOBE BRYANT (2003)

This is a classic case of "telling" more than snitching because bitch-ass Kobe did not have to do it. He was so scared of losing his ultra-sexy young wife that he would have done anything. So then, why did he bend that white bitch over a chair and screw her from behind while he was supposed to be under doctor's care in Colorado Springs?

The story goes like this:

> When interrogated about his 2004 Colorado rape allegations, **Kobe sold his then teammate, the hulking Shaquille O'Neal, up the river and probably ruined Shaq's marriage in the process.** Bryant stated that "he should have done what Shaq does and pay his women not to say anything." He stated Shaq has paid "up to a million dollars already." Way to throw the big guy under the bus. (Shelton, 2015)

Needless to say, Shaq's wife was pissed. Do you think Kobe gave a shit? Shaq stated openly that Kobe's "snitching" paved the way for the end of his (Shaq's) marriage. As it was reported in the Daily Mail,

> Kobe Bryant was on the receiving end of a withering Shaq attack the other night as his former teammate trashed him as a no-good home wrecker. Phoenix Suns center Shaquille O'Neal, who has a long-running feud with his ex-Lakers teammate, took the mic at the Village Underground Sunday and unleashed his tirade. "I'm a horse, Kobe ratted me out, that's why I'm getting divorced," Shaq rapped. **The line refers to a comment Bryant made during his 2003 rape case in which he told Colorado cops that he should have done what Shaq does: "Shaq would pay his women not to say anything."** (Piazza, 2008 – emphasis added)

So because he assaulted a white girl and the white girl snitched on HIM (and got paid in an out of court settlement), he turns the tables on another black man and punks him out in order to divert attention. There are varying degrees of snitching and this is that street-level type – the kind that makes young bruthas from one crew take a gun and head over to a competing gang member and bust a cap. That's a lot of what is taking place in Omaha and its spate of black male shootings. More on that later in this book.

JIMMY HENCHMAN (2011)

Speaking of young black males, here is a story about a Millennial snitch:

> In 2011, the FBI indicted hip-hop mogul James "Jimmy Henchman" Rosemond on charges that he ran a $10 million a year drug ring. **According to authorities, that's when he started naming names in exchange for time shaved off his inevitably lengthy sentence.** Henchman reportedly detailed aspects of his operation and admitted to prosecutors that the majority of his income was derived from illegal means. (Shelton, 2015 – emphasis added)

He took the Sammy Gravano route: when your ass is in a sling, tell on a bunch of other people and divert attention from your crimes and at the same time serve less time. And telling on himself and a few others wasn't all that this "negro" did:

> He also admitted to **loaning Wyclef Jean drug money and selling the rapper's driver several kilos of dope,** as well as using Interscope's offices do make drug drops. (Shelton, 2015 – emphasis added)

The more the snitches talk, the longer the list grows. The longer the list grows the more control the system has over the lives of those that have been "targeted." That is how the snitch system works and that is why so many people are passive and quiet; they don't want to involve their relatives and friends with the federal government because everybody knows how duplicitous and two-faced the government has been and can be.

The ultimate "reward" for snitching and helping out the government can best be seen in the existence of the Witness Protection Program, which is explored in the next section of this book.

Notes and a Primer on Cops, Crime and "The Capture"

Most crime is "organized" in my view. And since the police are more or less buffoons who rely on public information, confidential informants and their pitifully under-documented "data systems," they need to fear those entities that fall under the label of "organized crime" because they know what it means. Organized crime and snitches work hand in hand, which is why those who have truly "organized" crime families are closely knit and they truly pride the concept of loyalty. To betray that loyalty is punishable by death. Read later about what recently happened to Whitey Bulger.

A book titled *What cops know: Today's police tell the inside story of their work on America's streets.* (New York: Pocket Books) by Connie Fletcher (1990) was the source of a book I wrote under another title. But there is information about cops and how they think and act that is important in order for us to better understand any local "snitch system" and its relationship to the system, in general.

In December 2001 it was reported that a police group, known as "Area 2" was under investigation because a death row inmate claimed that detectives tortured him to extract a false confession. In 1986, the story goes, officers in the unit suffocated Aaron Patterson with a plastic typewriter cover until he confessed to the murder of an elderly couple. Lieutenant Jon Burge headed the special unit and was fired in 1993 after another inmate was also found to have been tortured into making a false confession (Injuryboard.com, 2001).

By the way, Burge's reign as a Chicago Police Commander was so vicious it was the subject of a videotape titled, "The End of the Nightstick: Confronting Police Brutality in Chicago." The tape shows the cover-ups, institutional racism and violence that were all conducted on Burge's watch. For twenty years the press and authorities turned a deaf ear to allegations of what Burge and his Cronies were doing. Evidently, Dr. Fletcher chose to do the same thing.

Fast forward to May of 2001, where the City of Chicago settles a wrongful death lawsuit because, on June 4, 1999, Chicago cops shot down unarmed LaTanya Haggerty (Paulsen, 1999: 5). The city had to pay out $18 million. By the way, the day following the June 4th shooting of Ms. Haggerty, a young brother named Robert Russ was pulled over for a tragic stop. One officer used his gun to smash in the rear driver's –side window and then shot him dead (Paulsen, 1999: 5).

In November of 2000, Office Charles Bowery of the Chicago Police Department committed suicide because he found out he was the target of a probe for allegedly shaking down Polish immigrants on Chicago's northwest side; more specifically, Jefferson Park neighborhood (Cop Crime Links, 2000). How do you think he was found out? Somebody snitched, that's how. I'm willing to bet that his fellow cops knew all along and, as they tend to do, just kept quiet.

In Chicago, the cops have plenty of help from the system, in general (a point that I make later in this book). Chicago has, for more than a century, been steeped in corruption, from the street level cop and political "bossism" to the precinct captains to the Cook County judges. Look at the September

26, 1997 case of young Jeremiah Mearday as it was reported in the April 2, 1998 issue of *Worker's World* newspaper:

> Jeremiah Mearday would not keep silent after two Chicago cops brutally attacked him last Sept.26. Police officers Matthew Thiel and James Comito had stopped the 18-yearold African American without reason, then beaten him with heavy flashlights. After months of mass struggle, the Chicago Police Board was forced to announce March 12 that Thiel and Comito would be fire. One week later, on March 20, cops from the same district grabbed Mearday off the front steps of his home. According to witnesses Mearday shouted, "Why are you doing this to me?" as the police threw him t the ground, handcuffed him and wrestled him into the patrol car (Worker's World, 1998).

Continuing:

> At the station, police searched Mearday's clothes and shoes. They then returned these items to him. Cops later took Mearday's shoes a second time. This time, police claimed to find cocaine in his shoes. Mearday now faces new charge of drug possession and assaulting police. The trumped- up charges from Sept. 26 were never dropped. A witness in the neighborhood contradicted the police version of the arrest. These witnesses were served with subpoenas to appear before a grand jury on March 23. It is unprecedented for witnesses to be summoned to a grand jury with no notice and no time to get legal representation. The Fraternal Order of Police has mobilized up to 150 police officers to attend Mearday's court appearances (Worker's World, 1998; Robinson, 1998).

Rallying police power to go to court to intimidate the public; beating black people up; planting drugs on citizens. And, of course, setting up elaborate snitch systems so that you can browbeat, bribe and brutalize people on the street in exchange for information. This is the reality that the white majority in America doesn't want to hear about.

Furthermore, this is not the first time you've heard this, I am sure. But Dr. Fletcher had to know it and instead of dealing with it through interview, inquiry and research, she allows the cops and detectives in her book to tell THEIR version as if it is the only version. This then, forced citizens like me to have to take out time and present the other side, since it is clear that the pro-police scholar Fletcher did not see the need to do it.

Remember the night the Chicago Bulls won the 1998 NBA championship? Well, while the city of Chicago was partying – including Dr. Fletcher no doubt – several black motorists was shot and wounded by Chicago cops. Tapes of police radio conversations were discovered in which cops said, "Don't call an ambulance – let them bleed to death." Who "discovered" the radio conversations?

Doesn't Ms.Fletcher remember these incidents and why weren't either of them mentioned in the section under "violent crimes"? Or is it that violent crimes only count when they are committed by the citizenry, and not when committed by out-of-control police officers?

Had Ms. Fletcher conducted some serious research – which I am sure she instructs her journalism students to do – she would have found information dating back to 1990 (her book was published in that year) that shows that these Chicago cops are trigger-happy. According to one source, "between 1990 and 1998, [Chicago] police recorded 505 shootings, including 139 deaths, OPS [Office of Professional Standards] records show. The largest number of fatalities – 21 – occurred in 1994" (Gordon, 1999). Of the 139 fatalities, 82 were black, 15 Latino, 12 whites and 2 Asians. Why didn't the "detectives" and cops being interviewed by Fletcher mention these little tidbits?

If the words and thoughts of these cops and detectives ring so true and are so valuable, then why did citizens in the city of Chicago – where Fletcher resides, no doubt – have to form the Greater Chicago Committee Against Police Brutality?

And I am sure that Fletcher is aware that since 1977, the Illinois criminal justice system *has had to free more than 20 death row inmates because of wrongful convictions* – most of those coming out of Chicago, and coming from the "arrests"and"investigations" conducted by members of the same police department that she now devotes an entire book to.

The cops and detectives that were interviewed by Fletcher had to ***know*** about some of these incidents – if indeed, not all of them. And, in particular, there is little doubt in my mind that these cops and detectives were well aware of the police-sponsored crimes and violations that took place in Chicago. It was probably locker room banter or a joke-a-minute exchange while riding in the police cruiser or with a pal in an unmarked cop car. Regardless of the context, news regarding police screw-up, brutality and harassment (and how they "got that nigger" or what they "did to that spic") fly fast among the men in blue. They apparently agree with such actions. As the case studies above show, there is almost a uniformity in the amount of greed, graft and grotesqueness that police get involved in.

That is why I find it ironic that the final sentence in this book is a question posed by a detective who has just described future crimes, claiming that "organ farming" – growing babies, killing them and then selling their various body parts – will take place on a global level. The final four words which make up the question, also apply to Ms. Fletcher in regard to why she wrote such a one-sided book, defending such a callous and cold-hearted group of people. The question is: ***doesn't that scare you?***

This book doesn't tell us very much that is valid at the street level. But it does give us a good idea of the thought processes of these policemen, and it is frightening that a group of people with so much power, and with so much responsibility thrust upon them could be, as a collective, so cold, calculating and downright stupid. Hence, the need for confidential informants, snitches, "stoolies" and the like.

Tom Bradley, former mayor of Los Angeles once said, "When decision-makers check their ethics at the door, there is not a chance in the world that their tough decisions will be tempered with moral concerns. This, I believe, is what's happening too often in our country, in our business life, in our community life, and in our political life." (Jet, 6-13-83: 32). In my view, this statement extends most definitely to the police departments around this country in general and to the members of the Chicago Police Department, in particular.

Connie Fletcher's book, because of its rambling, sometimes contradictory and oftentimes incorrect statements made by police officers, is more a reflection of a collection of commonly held beliefs, stereotypes and racist viewpoints. As such, analyzing their own words gives us a better idea of what cops THINK than what they actually KNOW. Knowledge should be based upon and rooted in experience and facts, not assumptions, wild conjecture and bullshit. And yet, all three of these permeate Connie Fletcher's book, which was a transcription of tape recordings from law enforcement officers from throughout Chicago's ranks.

One thing about "what cops know" is clear; these cops know how to "rank" certain crimes, certain classes of criminals, certain levels of criminal expertise and, in doing so, shroud their roles of crime fighters in cloaks of stupidity. And more importantly, intimidate the living hell out of hand chosen people to get them to "tell" on others, turn in their friend and associates and sell out anyone that the cops deem "a target."

Now you should be able to see why so few cases are solved; why crime is usually on the upswing; why there is a spate of what are referred to as "cold cases" – cases that have gone unsolved for so long that they are filed away. Now you can see the mentality and the attitudes of the men who are paid to solve these crimes.

Identifying these distinctions in "levels" of criminality, combined with the general stupidity of cops and detectives, are essentially just two major problems that I have with these cops and detectives interviewed for Connie Fletcher's book. In addition, there are a number of methodological differences between my approach to research and the approaches conducted by Ms. Fletcher. I should note that **Ms. Fletcher's Ph.D is in English Literature**, and all that requires is content analysis and some qualitative research. Very little critical reasoning involved, for the most part. In the case of this book and another book she wrote called **Pure Cops** (she has a third book where she talks to female cops), all she does is sashay in with a tape recorder, turn it on, and then type up a (poorly edited) draft of what was said.

I am essentially cleaning up Connie Fletcher's mess. She presents what the cops say as facts. I disagree with their claims, my disagreement rooted in and based on empiricism, experience in the streets and hard-core research. I believe that most of what the cops and detectives told Dr. Fletcher was nothing short of biased opinion and in some cases, outright lies. In this case, that's the difference between me and these cops that Fletcher is interviewing: they claim to be police officers and detectives and yet they have the same mentality as the people they are trying to capture.

By their own admission, these cops and detectives can "admire" someone who displays finesse as he's robbed someone of their worldly belongings; they can "appreciate" a "good hit" by a professional hit man; they can differentiate between someone who steals another person's dreams in the daytime and a rogue who does it at night. They can even hand pick and pay off those who they use as "CIs" (confidential informants).

White folks have been programmed to suspect and hold accountable "the other." That "other," in a nation as segregated as this one, is anyone who is not white. This "aryanized" thinking, therefore, enables the shrewd white con man to take advantage. And this is what you get: white boys raping their daughters (not the "colored beast" they've been programmed to fear); white bankers and corporate leaders bilking them out of billions (not the shrewd gypsy con artist); white folks conning them at every turn.

If we go by the contents of Fletcher's book, you can see where the cops and detectives act as if drug dealers could not possibly reside in a condo on Chicago's Gold Coast, but they take time out to talk about the roaches and grime and the abused children in ghetto homes that they invade. With the help of the white-controlled media, the drug dealer's image is akin to that of the rapist and criminal: dark skin, baseball cap on backwards, sagging pants, hanging on a corner shouting, "yo, yo, yo!" The real drug dealer is the white corporate executive and the politician and Washington who are flying it in and shipping it in via Florida, California and New York.

There is, in the final analysis, a most simple explanation to all of this contrariety: ***These cops are white men***. That explains their inherent biases, their intellectual inadequacies, their racism and their misogynistic views. And men of this ilk keep reproducing themselves; their racist networks, unions and "contacts" enable the worst of the worst to pass tests, get through the academy and then get on the street – armed to the teeth. How else to explain the intergenerational examples of police brutality, harassment and murders that take place in the ghetto and the barrio?

At the same time, Connie Fletcher is supposed to be a communications scholar, and yet nowhere in the book does she stand up for the people that these men verbally abuse throughout this book. She doesn't even say anything about these men referring to women as "broads" and "bitches." And I find it hard to believe that none of these racists used the word "nigger" in more than 900 police statements that appeared in the book. Perhaps she saw fit to edit it out or perhaps warned them.

One detective did admit there was "prejudice," a word they use because it s a lot less intense than "racism." Here is what this detective said on page 38 of the book:

> You'll find that a copper's prejudice is always directed at the poorest segment of the society where he serves. New York cops think Puerto Ricans are the scum of the earth. Out West, Southwest, the coppers know nothing about Puerto Ricans, blacks, Appalachian whites. THEY hate American Indians. In the Northwest, there are cops who hate ESKIMOS. And when you get coppers together, each one says to the cops from the other parts of the country, "Listen, you think Puerto Ricans are bad …'

A tell-tale quote if I ever heard one.

The key word in the preceding quote? "Hate." These are white men showing what makes them white. They have a disdain for everyone, and it's not based on what anyone has done to them personally; it's based on and rooted in their own racist attitudes about anyone who has skin color. In fact, these "cops" often abuse their own people, but that's another story. But one point about the passage that I would like to qualify.

Do not be duped into thinking that the white cop is a "geographic racist" or a "precinct bigot," as I call them. These cops hate ALL people of color, it's just that the ones that are closest to them are the ones that perturb them the most; the ones that they see most often with consenting white women; the ones that are confined to a certain part of the city that they (the cops) can easily patrol and abuse. As Frantz Fanon once wrote, "a racist in a culture of racism is therefore normal."

But at any rate, any editing done was selective and as I stated earlier about white discretion, it (discretion) almost always leads to some form of abuse of minorities.

I am afraid that Connie Fletcher assumed the role of "passive observer" during her interviews. It seems as if she just sat there with her tape recorder and allows them to spew forth their venom. In doing so, I believe she betrayed her obligation to academia, her fellow white women, women in general and to black folks, who may well one day wind up being the victims of these racist clowns, masquerading as cops and detectives.

Organized Crime

The chapter begins with an attempt at dismissing the myth of organized crime being only about the Italians. And in doing so, offers up a bit of history as well:

> Organized crime follows a military structure. You've got the bosses, the lieutenants, the soldiers. When they started in Italy, they formed it after the ancient Roman legions. They thought that was a good idea. The structure doesn't change; the players change. There's one or two bosses, five or six lieutenants, seventy made guys that we've identified, and about 318 who work for them; that's their sole income; they don't have any other income. Each boss has his own bookkeeper. Some are former IRS agents, others are Outfit CPAs (p. 310).

I'm willing to bet that the majority of those accountants, as was the case during the days of Capone, are Jews.

Continuing:

> Organized crime is not all Banlon shirts and patent-leather shoes. That's the first thing intelligence detectives will tell you. "The problem with organized crime is everybody looks at it as if you're just looking at Italians. But 'organized crime,' just as a general term, is any organized unit that's committing crimes," as Chief Investigator Jerry Gladden of the Chicago Crime Commission put it. It's divided into what they call traditional organized crime: the Outfit, La Cosa Nostra, the Mafia, the various criminal offshoots of Prohibition that have dominated not only U.S. crime, but unions, businesses, professions, and government for decades …
> (p. 294)

How could a country not steeped in criminal intent and founded by the scum of the earth not be a giant manifestation of "organized crime"? What about the U.S. government and its racist invasions, its color-oriented wars, its massacres of entire nations of people, its legacy of slavery and Jim Crow, and its on-going abuse of women, the disabled and people of color? There are too many incidents for us to write off this collective deviance as some kind of quirk or accident. No, it is "organized" and yes, it is quite "criminal."

Don't forget that we also have,

> … nontraditional organized crime, the criminal groups coming up in a big way, including the Colombians, the Cubans, the Japanese, Yakuza, (sic) Jamaican posses, and street gangs, that have evolved into enormous criminal enterprises, like the El Rukns, the Crips, the Bloods (p. 294).

And with skin color comes the inevitable stereotypes of savagery and brutality. Toward the end of the chapter, one cop puts it this way:

> Organized crime – it's not the big bad tiger of the jungle anymore. There's other tigers out there – with different stripes. Some of the nontraditional organized crime groups coming up now make the Outfit guys look like wimps. In their methodology, they certainly do. And some of them have been around a lot longer — the Japanese Yakuza, for example, have been dealing with the WORLD, moving money, for more than forty years. The nontraditional criminals make the Outfit look wimpy,

> in both nastiness AND power … [T]he Yakuza, the
> Japanese, get into this [ritualistic procedures]. They're
> into tattooing and mutilation. You tattoo your body and
> cut of one of your fingers. Why would they do that? To
> defeat infiltration (pp. 332-333).

Notice that in the cop description of the second group, all of the "subjects" are people of color for the most part or, at very least, hail from countries where the majority population is either black, brown or yellow. That is probably what that cop meant when he alluded to a "tiger with different stripes." The fact is, when the white man, with his discretion combined with his racist history, makes such divisions, it is no quirk; by his own admission he has divided it into two groups. Why? Because Italians are considered white, that's why. If crime is crime no matter who commits it, then why divide manpower up that way?

Why not use information that the Italians have provided, including their structure and methods (which most of these colored groups have studied, anyway) to get a jump on the groups of color? There can be but one racism: The Mafia and the Italians have internal connections and political connections (which you will read about later in this section) and the other groups, because they are of color, do not.

And one last point: even when the Italians are portrayed or perceived as kingpins and criminals, it is in a more respectful way than any other criminal group. They are viewed as united, intelligent and clean. In most cases their hatred of black people is made most apparent. And yet terms like "first," "successful," "clever" and other positive adjectives are used in describing them. For example:

> Italian organized crime, the bad Boys' success story,
> shows where a perverse profit motive can lead. As the
> first and signally (sic) triumphant organized crime
> movement in the United States, the Outfit may serve as a
> beacon to groups coming up and a distress signal to the
> rest of us – the worst may be yet to come (p. 298).

How could the "worst be yet to come" when the Italians have a history and legacy of death and destruction in their wake? When their very presence threatens the nature of the political system that governs America? When they are the "crime standard" for all other groups? By saying the worst is yet to come is to give a "pass" to the Italians and to underestimate their impact on every aspect of this society.

How can "the worse" be "yet to come" when the cops have information, insight and evidence that the Italians have their internal murder codes, strategies and tactics on, not only how to handle murdering regular targets, but even their own people? Let's take a look at the following information and see if "the worst is yet to come."

One cop explains, as follows:

> Organized-crime murders aren't like ordinary murders. Roughly 70 percent of all murders in the United States are domestic murders, which means it's a husband killing a wife or a wife killing a husband, or a boyfriend or a girlfriend. There's some family or sexual relationship. The killer is known to the victim, and the victim is known to the killer ... Organized crime murders, however, have all the elements that are necessary to confuse and stymie law enforcement people. One, the killer is probably not personally known to the victim. Two, the motive may not be immediately clear. Three, there's some planning. These are not spur-of-the-moment crimes. Now, there will always be an exception, but for the most part ... it's something that's planned (pp. 314-315).

Continuing:

> The Outfit plans its murders ahead of time. How good the plan is, of course, depends upon the people who are carrying the murder out. Some of them are quite good and invest a considerable amount of time in their planning. They'll stake the individual out. They'll do a surveillance. They know where he lives, they know where he works, they'll determine his route home, what time he leaves, what time he arrives. And they're always looking for the opportunity – where is he when he has the least number of people around?—where is he isolated? Where is he out of his car? And if they have the time, they will pick the best time and place (pp. 315-316).

This is the ideal bureaucracy, a smooth running corporation that has police on their payroll, politicians in their pockets and an international reputation. They have interlocking directorates just like any other corporation. And then there are the outright networks that can be used to make any "hit" tantamount to the "perfect crime:"

So the planning is there. Now the other thing that helps considerably is not only the planning, but utilizing the criminal network to provide them with the things that the ordinary guy can't get. And that's the stolen car that can't be traced except to the legitimate owner. Stolen firearms that can't be traced. With an Outfit murder, the car can be seen; it doesn't make any difference ... The planning that goes into stalking a guy and picking the spot. Sometimes there's a tail car involved, a driver, a couple of gunmen, walkie-talkies, CB radios used for communication (p. 316).

Then there's the "after-action," as one cop called it:

There's a place they're going afterwards. There's check-off lists: "Did you get rid of this?" "Did you get rid of that?" Sometimes the guys immediately responsible leave town. The reservations, the tickets. All that has to be planned. And by the time you find the body, the hitmen may be on a plane to Vegas, or Timbuktu. It's always a stranger who hits a stranger ... They know exactly what his next move is gonna be. What his weakness is, his strong points ... A good hit is a piece of art. A lot of crimes are works of art. A good burglary, a good stickup, a good hit (pp. 316-317).

Works of art? These Chicago cops are sick. If a hit can be a work of art, and a stickup – taking somebody's stuff at gunpoint – can be a work of art, are we to assume that the decades-long rapes of little boys by Catholic priests are also works of art because the priests escaped detection? How about Jeffrey Dahmer's murders of 17 men of color? Was that a work of art because he got away with it for so long and across state lines? These cops compliment organized crime personnel because they envy them. On page 318, a cop says, "There's always a touch of class to Outfit hits. A lot of planning goes into them, unless it's an emergency." A touch of class? How about when they go after their own?

That's right. Unlike black folks – who seem to reward and forgive our traitors – the Italians (and any other group worth its salt) go about the business of punishing their turncoats. One cop posits,

Usually, someone in the organization is hit because quite often they're found o be cheating. Or there's a criminal investigation and they feel that this guy's cooperating and

> he's going to jeopardize a boss. Most of the guys that go
> in front of a federal grand jury and who can't sleep the
> night before and who are trembling and sweating
> profusely are too worried about the federal grant jury.
> What they're worried about is when they get called over
> to have a chat with someone and the guy sits there and
> asks, "You didn't tell them anything, didju, Tony?"

If only our leaders, at any level, feared the wrath of the masses in such a manner! Continuing:

> People will kill to send messages … There's different
> ways to get hit. Basically, having your head blown off is
> an honorable way to go. An immediate kill shows
> respect ….If they think the guy's an informant, they do
> some things. Cut off his penis, stick it in his mouth, let
> him bleed to death. Kill him with an ice pick. Slowly.
> Cut him from the ear to the mouth. That's the kind of
> bodies we find of people that we believe they suspected
> to be informants. That's the way they were disfigured –
> as opposed to a guy who just screwed up (p.322).

In my view, Chicago's cops identify with these mobsters because of the immigrant history of that city. At one point, all of their ancestors lived in slums and then, as they moved out, blacks moved in. But because these white immigrants had white skin and were willing to kiss the ass of the American white man, they were able to secure some political power which, in turn, enabled them to curry favor with the ward bosses which, in the final analysis, opened up some doors for them. Once these white immigrants got in – the Irish, the Slavs, the Italians, the Jews – they slammed the door tight and made sure no people of color would get in.

The white Chicago cop of today is an extension of the white immigrant experience. And at one time, they all had their hands in some kind of illegal activity: drugs, alcohol, prostitution. Then, when they win some rights, they turn around the shut down the black-run after hours joints, the black gambling shacks and the black prostitution business in the name of "justice" and "community morals."

You will recall earlier in this chapter on "organized crime" it was alleged that "the worst is yet to come." Can people of color or any other group be as cold and callous as these wise guys?

Furthermore, as you will see, these "organized crime types" usually have the cops and the politicians in their back pocket. They are "connected," as the following information bears out:

> Most of U.S. organized crime itself is buried now, embedded in legitimate business and government. Organized crime lies deep, says one investigator: "The crime syndicate well fall apart the day when you read in the papers that we've walked in and we've served subpoenas on three quarters of the city council and we've gone into the Congress of the United States and we've done the same thing. Because they have somewhere in their political history, passed a law, gotten involved in some transaction, accepted donations to their fund, or shared in insider information that came from the Outfit –some had no idea they were getting tied into the Outfit; others did it ***knowingly*** (pp. 295-296).

I think it is a lie to believe that a skilled politician would not know if he was involved with organized crime. But if the writer knows those who are associated and who know they are, why haven't these politicos been busted? Do you see the double standard?

But this only proves all the more how racist America is and how its police divisions – paid for with black tax dollars as well as white – are just as racist as the other institutional arrangements in this country. Back to organized crime and the fact that Chicago's version has a reputation that is rather unique. One cop put it this way:

> Other organized crime groups in the country think the Chicago Outfit is crazy. The word is. "Stay away from them. They're not normal." Chicago's always had the renegades. It goes back to Capone. You know, one time two New York guys were sent to kill Capone. They were met at the train and beaten to death. Part of their bodies were sent back on the train to New York with a note: "Don't send boys to do a man's job." The Chicago Outfit is ***the*** Outfit. It's the most powerful individual organization in the U.S. I believe that there's no other monolithic structure with as much power and control and money as the Chicago Outfit (p.308).

Put another way, "The Chicago Outfit has never, ever been stuck with a provincial mentality. The Outfit is a monolithic, single-minded structure that has always believed that it didn't stop at the Chicago River. The Outfit's *everywhere.* And there's enough, as we say in Chicago, for everybody (p. 310).

Continuing:

> The secret to their success, which remains a secret today, is when you go someplace and you represent Chicago interests, that's what you do. And I don't care if you stay there for thirty years and think you have your own empire, you are controlled by the Chicago Outfit, and that's where your allegiance goes. And when you forget about it, they kill you. Chicago has a stranglehold, it has complete, utter domination over major unions – and the major unions we're talking about are groups like the Teamsters and the Produce Drivers. That's Chicago (p. 309).

I think I can see what's going on here. These Chicago cops see themselves as a part of the "elite" just because their city is great, because the city's ambience is internationally recognized and, after all, it is the second largest city in the nation (Los Angeles might have something to say about that). So when they recall stories about Capone and the days of Prohibition, when they hear about movies like "Goodfellas," "The Godfather" and "The Untouchables," these asshole cops – most of whom don't even live in the city but who, indeed, live in the suburbs – think that they are somehow making history or that they're superheroes. Former mobster Sam Giancana's favorite song was Sinatra's, "Chicago, My Kind of Town."

As far as black folks are concerned, there are two versions of "the Outfit;" one is the guys in blue with the billy clubs, the dogs and the mace. The other one is made up of the guys who like spaghetti and whose last names end in a vowel. Both are accepted versions of what has come to be known as "organized crime."

Black folks are some of the biggest backers of organized crime that there are in this country. How? Through their support of the casinos, "going to play the ponies," "bettin' on the dogs," and other forms of gambling, that's how. As one detective explains it,

> Gambling is still organized crime's biggest money-maker. Just the sheer volume of business You got a big football weekend coming up – you know there's gonna be a lot of bookmaking on sports betting. Just millions of dollars are spent on sports betting. And horse races, that's

the other part of the backbone of gambling, it's just a constant (p. 300).

Continuing:

> And the workers, the guys actually taking the bets, they've been arrested, maybe hundreds of times – it doesn't mean anything to them; it's just the cost of doing business, it's just part of the scheme, you know? They get out on bond, nobody gets too excited about it, and they never go to jail. You know where they have the biggest illegal bookmaking operations? Right on racetracks. You know why? Because people can get credit from their bookie. You can't get credit at the windows; you've gotta have the money (pp. 300-301).

So the cops know all this – and yet organized crime continues and, in fact, expands. What does this say about the cops? Either they're incompetent as hell, they're afraid or they're involved in the criminal activities themselves.

In point of fact, gambling gives rise to other forms of deviant activity – like loan sharking:

> With gambling automatically comes juice. The average on juice loans now is 5 to 10 percent a week till the debt is paid off. And if you don't pay it, the juice accumulates. They like to call in the entire note every once in a while, then they'll loan it right back to you just to make sure you're not blowing it. So if you borrowed $165,000, your interest per week is $16,500. And maybe you didn't even keep up with the juice payments. So that adds on to the principal, so now you have 10 percent on to whatever ads on. So if you run it up to $200,000, now it's $20,000 a week. And it just goes up. It might be millions. And eventually they just take over your business, and you wind up being a collector for ***them*** (p. 302).

It gets even deeper:

> Gamblers go to loan sharks. People who can't get money through legitimate sources go to loan sharks. Deadbeats. Some businessmen. High-line burglars. You know, "I want to get into this thing that's gonna get me three hundred thousand dollars. I need fifty thousand

dollars to buy equipment." Then they share in the
profits (p. 302).

The key word is "share."

Don't forget; these cops know where all this "sharing" is taking place. And they know who is doing it. Why don't they conduct a raid and take the money under asset forfeiture laws? Because organized crime has them in their pocket, that's why. Not only that, but it is the white businessman, the successful businessman, that is taking out these loans. And with the economy being what it is, who knows how many friends of the police department these businessmen employ?

The Italians, like the Jews, keep it in the family. In fact, that's what La Cosa Nostra means – "our thing." They can borrow from each other, buy from each other, cover for one another and, when needed, get the help of an Italian whose on the inside. Black folks are always under scrutiny; how can we infiltrate anything when it's lily-white and racist? Some Italians are so white that all they have to do is change their last name. Perry Como did. Dean Martin did.

We, as black folk, call each other "brother" and "sister" but when it comes to long range planning and structure, we don't act very brotherly or sisterly. Imagine if we did? Imagine if we had bail bondsmen in place, black people on the police force who were really black; imagine if we had blacks who were judges and wardens. Imagine we had black lawyers who gave a damn? Imagine if we had black hospital administrators, blacks who were in charge of media assignments and black politicians who cared about their constituents? Not only would this cut back on our social vulnerability, but these incomes and statuses would play a major role in black economic development, role modeling for future generations and impacting on short- and long-term social policy.

But it is this kind of unity that paves the way for long-term investments, even if they do come from a loan shark. But it's a life-or-death business in some cases, as explained on page 303 of Fletcher's book:

> They [loan sharks] put the squeeze on you. The juice can
> be any amount, 50, 75, even a 100 percent. It mostly
> depends on the amount borrowed. There are cases where
> you borrow $100, you gotta give back $200, those are
> very sort-term kinds of things. You keep paying.
> Obviously, they don't have any written contract; this
> isn't like the General Motors Acceptance Corporation.
> So even if you've paid it all back, they can come to you,

> and they do, and say, "You still owe … They extend it
> as long as they want to extend it. So it gets to a point
> where it's an extortion more than a repayment of a loan.

Such arrangements are not unique to Italians; Jews did the same thing to black people when they operated small shops in black communities. It was more subtle, there was hardly a hint of violence, but the end result was the same: loan sharking and threats of taking blacks to court where the Jew would inevitably win. To this very day, The both the Italian and the Jew continue to operate "pawn shops" and "jewelry and loan" businesses in low-income areas. It appears that the police know what is going on – even to the point where these people purchase stolen goods – and yet they [the police] do nothing.

According to the cops in this book, times have changed when it comes to the Italians – they're more serious with their loans now:

> They used to break your thumbs or break a kneecap with
> a baseball bat if you were behind in your juice payments.
> They don't do that anymore. You have to pay or you die.
> Bosses don't want to be in and out of federal court with
> threatening people, and going back, and by then the
> guy's wearing a wire. If you've got him up so tight that
> there's nowhere else for him to go but the government,
> he's gonna go, and he's gonna wear a wire. If he owes
> and he won't pay, you want to set an example, you just
> kill him. Make your payments (p. 303).

According to one cop, "there are more adult bookstores in the United States of America than there are McDonald's hamburger stores" (p. 304). And it is for this reason that the Outfit controls pornography:

> Let's put it this way: If you were going to go into
> business selling pornography, you would certainly be
> associated with organized crime. If you weren't directly
> involved with organized crime—if they didn't front the
> money for you to open this business and if they didn't
> come to you and try to extort money from you for ***doing***
> the business – then at least you would be associated with
> organized crime because you would be getting your
> material from distributors who are either ***controlled*** or
> ***owned*** organized crime!. Somewhere along the line,
> through distribution or sales, they're gonna get their
> piece of the action (p. 304).

This is the same thing the Jews did during the early days of the movie industry: they controlled the distribution, they controlled the celluloid material that the film was made on and, in that way, there was no way you could make a film without going through the Jews. Again, we see a similarity, with the Jews being more covert and duplicitous in their dealings while Italians are more up front with theirs.

At any rate, "the biggest money maker for the Outfit in porno is videos." Continuing:

> In adult bookstores, peep shows are the biggest money makers. They make the Outfit an incredible amount of money. You go in and just keep paying to keep the show going. They either give you some tokens for the coin-op, or they give you some Susan B. Anthony dollars. The only use that's ever been found for the Susan B. Anthony dollar is to keep peep shows going – that's kind of ironic. … (p. 304).

Interesting how cops talk about porno but never mention how they buy bootie from prostitutes. They don't talk about how they force women to give them head or else threaten to "run them in." They don't talk about how they meet streetwalkers after work as is the case in both Omaha and Milwaukee, and then after getting some head, they tear up the ticket.

Earlier, I mentioned mob movies and the role that Jews played in the early days of Hollywood. Well guess what: The Italians are involved in Tinseltown as well. As described on page 310,

> The Chicago Outfit controls the unions. Because of that, they're into everything. Chicago controls a big chunk of Hollywood. They don't' control the corporations, they don't control the directors and the producers per se, they don't control the actors and actresses. But all the support – all the catering, the lighting, fixtures – the outfit that supplies stuff for the movies is not going to be an accidental supply house.. The lighting and fixtures – and everything that moves and walks and talks to cause that movie to be produced –is probably going to be owned outright or by a fictitiously formed blind trust by members of the Outfit (p. 310).

Throughout this section of this book, I have mentioned a parallel between what the Italians have done and what the Jews have done; I have also mentioned how, indeed, the Jews worked closely with the Italians during the early days of organized crime, with the Jews operating mainly as the bookkeepers and, of course, as the morticians while the Italian mobsters sent them plenty of corpses.

In addition to the union involvement and the areas already mentioned, these Chicago cops claim that the Outfit is into arson-for-profit. In that city it's not the junkie on the corner who the city hires to burn down a warehouse so they can save the cost of having it razed. These Outfit guys are on the inside. One cop claims, "I remember one guy, Tony Geronda, he worked for the City of Chicago, bureau of Streets and Sanitation, and he was also a bomber and an arsonist for the Outfit" (p. 307).

Some sources say that the mob doesn't mess with drugs. But I remember a line from the movie, "The Godfather," where some of the men were told to sell drugs only to "the niggers" because "they (blacks) have lost their souls." The way the cops tell it, some are into narcotics, others are not:

> They have some people that are dabbling in narcotics, and making big money, that start fooling around with young girls and then they will start sniffing themselves, and the next thing you do, you find them in a trunk. Every one of these men has a wife, has a respectable family, and a girlfriend on the side … That's accepted practice. If you have a girlfriend for twenty years, and some of them do, and all of a sudden you are fooling around with four, five young coke addicts, they're afraid of you. That's when you're signing your own death warrant. Narcotics, they were always reluctant because that brings a lot of heat. They didn't stay out because of any ethical scruples (p. 306).

<u>Oh yes they did!</u> They could have had it all and, in fact, they get involved on a selective basis. The Italians DO have scruples when it comes to drugs. The cops are just jealous because they know that if the Italians went hog wild over drugs, they would make mistakes which would make it easier for them to get busted; that would be a feather in the cap of the cops. So they lie and try to paint a negative picture of organized crime (a group that, in my view, has more scruples than the big-city cops do) – like the cop does in the following statement:

> I'm telling you this as a policeman. As someone whose been a policeman most of his life and is a policeman body and soul. I'm telling you that there is no honor. And that

is all Hollywood bullshit. There's no honor – The Godfather is all crap – these are a bunch of vicious … animals. They don't sit around and say, "Gee, you know, we gotta hit Tony – he's been a great guy. It's really a shame. Let's give Tony a nice send-off. And what we'll do, we'll shoot him right in the head to make it nice and quick." There are people in this business who are disturbed. There are people in this business who are sociopaths. I personally know of one hitman who I believe to be a serial killer who's simply found a way to vent his homicidal tendencies. There's no honor. I never get too excited when they're killing one another. You know, some scumbag gets knocked off by the Outfit, I can't get excited …And the do some horrible things to people (p. 324).

Let's dissect the preceding conniption fit point-by-point.

This cop says he has been a policeman all his life. Then as far as blacks and other minorities are concerned, he has been associated with a different form of "organized crime;" a legal form! How can he point the finger at the Outfit when his "outfit" murders more African-American men than all of the Mafia groups COMBINED.

How can a cop talk about having no honor? Is the "blue fraternity" supposed to be an example of honor? Ask people of color, from the young ones on up to the elders, what they think of the police. Ask this group to think of words that come to mind when they think of the word "police." I guarantee you the word, "honor" would not be a word you would hear.

The cop says that the movie, "The Godfather" is "all crap" and that "these people are animals." This man sounds like he has issues, in general. The Godfather is not "all crap;" there may be scenes that were exaggerated and there may be parts that irked this particular cop. But to say it is "all crap" is to generalize and that is one of the many problems these policemen have: the generalize. And then, he proceeds to do it again when he says, "these people are animals." Do all of them fit that description? Or is he putting all members of the Outfit into a neat bag that he can then hate?

All crap? What about the high-profile beating of Lenard Clark in Chicago, a beating supposedly administered by organized crime figure Frank Caruso? The only witness against Caruso, a mobster's son himself, was Michael Cutler. And guess what happened to him? He was shot to death on May 14, 1998 in the 5900 block of West Erie in the Austin neighborhood? The Chicago Times reported in May of 2003 that a judge, a legislator, police and prosecutors all said the killing by two hooded men had appeared to be a mob hit (Main, 2003: 10). What did Clark do? He was a black kid who made the mistake of venturing into Caruso's mostly white neighborhood, Bridgeport, on a bike! All crap? I don't think so.

Nebraska State Senator Ernie Chambers perhaps summed it up best: "White people, in general, do not like black people, in general." "Racism is alive and well. Mark my words. In spite of all the tragic nonsense about reverse discrimination, reverse racism and preferential treatment for Blacks, the only thing this world will give you because you are Black, is a hard time" (Dr. Samuel DuBois Cook, Jet, 10-10-83:39).

This is the conventional wisdom across communities of color in America, and it is based on what far too many cops do to blacks, American Indians and Latinos. "Those people" – that's what they say when they "patrol" the reservation, the ghetto and the barrio. That is why more than 60% of the people in prison are men of color, and why most of the victims of police shootings are black or Latino. The cops stereotype men of color, they make generalizations based on limited knowledge only.

Another point important to make here is how the cops in big cities often harass the homeless and, in particular, the mentally ill who are on the streets. According to a July Justice Department report, 16 percent of all prisoners, or about 283,000 people, are mentally ill. Another 547,000 mentally ill people are in the parole system" (Catalinotto, 1999: 3). The more powerless the group, the greater the degree of stigma society and cops impose on them and, in turn, the greater degree of harassment heaped upon them by police officers and detectives.

This cop quoted earlier, like many of his colleagues, placed the Outfit into an entirely different category of humanity – just as they do ALL blacks and ALL Latinos. Because most of these men are not the smartest people in the world to begin with, it is easy for them to fall prey to stereotyped thinking because of their limited intelligence and the fact that they believe that they are somehow "saviors" of society. This cop talks about there being men in the Outfit who are sociopaths, but what do you call it when no matter where you go in America, the leading victims of police shootings are black and Latino? Are we to believe that every single one of those incidents was a "righteous shoot?"

This cop talks about a "hitman" who he believed was a serial killer and was using the job as a way to vent his homicidal tendencies. Why aren't "theories" like this advanced when it comes to the white cops who continue to harass, beat and shoot down black folks? Why don't fellow officers tell the brass about the cop that's out there calling blacks "niggers" and Latino's "wetbacks" and goading young minority kids every chance he gets? Isn't HE the one venting? And doesn't such maltreatment of people that you don't even know constitute the basis for a sociopathic personality type?

Then he has the nerve to say, in a nutshell, that he doesn't care if members of the Outfit kill one another. But I have a feeling that this mentality also extends to blacks; they know that black-on-black crime is high, so perhaps they just lay back (after instigating, of course) and then come in to sweep up the mess. I've written extensively on this elsewhere, and I've quoted cops who make this precise statement. Once you successfully designate the "out group" as "they," then you can define them as evil, degenerate, dirty – whatever you want. And once you do that, you can justify whatever you do to them. After all, in your view, "they're not quite human."

According to another one of the cops being interviewed by Fletcher, "the whole business of the Italian Mafia and the blood oath and all that stuff, it probably did exist, and it makes great movie copy. But when you get right down to it, the bottom line has always been "Where's the money?" (p. 312).

I don't believe this because in order to be a "made man," you've got to be Italian. Even the cops know that:

> Organized crime in America *is* Italian. But the Italians in general take a bum rap. It's their tragedy. You know, 99.99 percent of Italian Americans are everything you should be in America. They're hardworking – they're doctors, they're lawyers, they're policemen, they're FBI agents, they're teachers. They take the rap for a handful of people (p. 313).

That's sticking to tradition, isn't it? And if this tradition is still intact, then that qualifies the earlier statement about the bottom line; while ""where's the money" might be the bottom line *financially,* the background of the person deciding who the bottom line will include and who will stay in charge of writing the contract that the bottom line appears on, will remain being determined by ethnicity and nationality. This, in my view, is rooted in the concept of ***Italianisimo.***

But the white American and the white ethnic have something in common: similar degrees of colorlessness. And they all hail from somewhere in Europe. They respect that. That is why in the earlier excerpt, you saw this cop, probably white, defending the "good Italians," willing to go out on the line and vouch for "99.99 percent" of the group. There is not a white cop that would go on record and state that 99.99% of blacks or Latinos were hard working because we are the ones that they are arresting, justifiably or not. But remember, America is not a meritocracy and it is racist: they watch out for each other – and they are "on guard" against the races they fear most: people of color.

> element involved – the Greek element is every bit as vicious and cruel as any Italian Outfit guy. It's like the Jews and Greeks are operating in their own territory, but they cooperate –it's like two countries getting along. They're part of the Outfit, and they cooperate because they're a much smaller community. They operate within their community, but they pay their dues … There are very few Irish in the Outfit; they don't' like to have anything to do with each other (pp. 312 & 313).

And because they are white before anything else, these "organized crime" people can infiltrate the system at all levels and, in doing so, watch the backs of their brothers who are actually calling the shots for the Outfit. They infiltrate the system in a myriad of ways and, in doing so, they perpetuate the Outfit's way of life. As one cop explained,

> They [organized crime] can't exist of and by themselves. One of the main reasons they **have** been able to exist is because they utilize middlemen. An organized crime figure cannot make a political contribution to an office-holder. That's anathema. He needs a clean middleman to be the guy to make the contribution, to be the guy to get somebody a job …. The Outfit couldn't exist if it couldn't compromise people. They're masters at corrupting. They've never been cheap when it comes to payoffs, to bribes. So you can't get mad at the Outfit without getting mad at whole other segments of society; at the hangers-on – people enjoy knowing mobsters, they like to be on the fringe. And then you've got to be mad at the corrupt officials, the corrupt lawyers, the corrupt police (p. 325).

Specifically, the infiltration of the police department. At a time when almost every city suffers from a shortage of minority officers and discriminates against the ones that DO apply, look at how the Outfits gets "their people" into the ranks of the boys in blue:

> Outfit coppers. Some young kid are told, "Why don't you go on the police department? You get some insurance and it's a good job, and we can take care of

> you there, we can help you out." And they do that. And then when they get on the job, they try and steer them toward units that they want them to be in, where they can help them: Gambling, Prostitution, Narcotics. The politicians make the clout calls for them (p. 325).

Not only that, but,

> There've been hitmen on the job. Guys who run gambling. Pickup men, burglars. I'm talking about organized crime burglars who work IN uniform, with squad cars. And then they take the organized crime regular burglar with them; they bring them, with the tools, in the squad car, and they're the lookout guys while the guy's in rooting the place. But these are rare animals; it's not a common thing (p. 325).

Bullshit. It's more common than this cop is willing to let one. Why? Two reasons. First of all, if he tells the truth, it shows the power that the Outfit has to infiltrate the ranks of cops. Secondly, if he tells the truth, it shows the role that cops are playing in perpetuating. crime. The fact that this cop talks about it in such detail, and knows of the existence of these kinds of collaborations taking place, shows that it is a successful endeavor and, as a result, has been repeated time and time again. Knowing about it doesn't mean that the burglar got caught; it means that the cops are out bragging about it or you hear about it through the cop grapevine. But the "blue fraternity" keeps you from telling what you know, illegal or not.

And in a society where black people who go by the book and work hard every day find it difficult to advance, these Outfit "infiltrators," courtesy of politicians on the take and other "inside help," can actually advance:

> A lot of Outfit guys are rewarded for illegal conduct with city jobs. We knew a guy who was a bouncer on Rush Street for a number of years. Then he went out with a guy and killed a guy. Thirty days later, he's just sitting, a tow-truck driver, $27,000 a year. When Jane Byrne was mayor, she got the word that there were some ghost payrollers at a city repair garage. So she told her driver one day —""go over here." Eight o'clock in the morning. Nobody knew she was coming, including her driver. She walked in, she wanted a roll call for all the

> workers, and she got other payroll sheets out. Fifty
> people were no-shows out of that one garage (p. 326).

This is yet another reason why the city administration of Chicago – and a multitude of other cities around the nation, no doubt – is so lacking in black and minority employees. How many members of the City Administrations of Omaha and Milwaukee, for example (two towns with major organized crime histories), are there in name only? How many are ghost payrollers? And at a time when all of America is upset about the lack of or inaccessibility to health care, these "cheaters" can get there through the Outfit:

> They like to get on the city payroll, the state payroll, for
> the hospitalization. They're like anybody else; they want
> their family covered. There's a lot of them working for
> the city and the state; that's the bottom of the rung, the
> soldiers. They never show up. It's a hustle (p. 326).

But the Outfits outreach spans beyond just cops, city jobs and health plans. The control is awesome:

> You've got them in the news media, you've got them in
> the state's attorney's office, you've got them in the
> police department. They're everywhere. They can
> always reach out to some contact they have. No one's
> exempt. Their real power is their influence and their
> favors-0owed formula. Because then they elicit the
> cooperation of people that are *not* organized crime. They
> are Outfit guys now that are general managers of major
> hotel chains; CEOs of major corporations that own hotel
> chains … (pp. 326-327).

Everywhere the Jews have power, the Italians have power. Why? Because it makes sense to use these kinds of tactics in order to advance your people. The only ones looking around to make OTHER groups powerful are black folk; all others are trying to get a piece of the rock for their people. But there is one difference between the Jews and the Italians as far as I can see: the Italians tend to use more force and are more into intimidation than the Jews. The Jews seem to be more cowardly and have others do their work for them. That's why the Jewish merchant is more likely to be a victim of the criminal "street tax" than any Italian businessman. Here's how the street tax works:

> They come to you. If you're doing anything illegal, they come to see you. It's more or less a dogma – you can't operate illegal businesses without paying your street tax to somebody. Gambling, cop shops, anything illegal. Pornography – the people who run pornography seem to think that that's legal because the Supreme Court said so. But the Outfit doesn't think so. So they extract the tax. You and I couldn't go into business and open a tavern and then start booking horses. Eventually, someone's gonna come knocking on the door. And they will find you. They have a better intelligence section than the police department … Somebody who won't pay the street tax when they tell him to pay, they just walk in and shoot him. Or take him for a drive and stick him in his own trunk (p. 308).

Street tax -- not a new concept. These white folks have been getting away with this for centuries. It still goes on in the larger cities, and the Italians still have it under control. In some parts of Los Angeles, I've heard, some brothers try to shake down the Korean grocers, but it never works. If the Italians find out that black folks are trying to assess a street tax, they take steps to make sure that it stops. This is only hearsay.

Then there's the escort services – a "business" that I always viewed as a front for prostitution rackets. Here's a story that one cop shares with the author, Fletcher:

> Of course, the Outfit is involved in escort services, of course they are. There's just too much money for them NOT to be. I've been told by two different services that one of their girls went on a date, got tied up, had a gun put to her head. This girl was told,"You tell So-and-so: Pay or you're going to start losing some girls." The services must have been making too much money and not paying the street tax to the Outfit. There was on really good escort service a couple years ago. A guy called them and said, "I want three girls." They sent up three girls, and he put a gun to the head of one girl. "Tell your boss he has a partner now." So now he's a partner" (p. 305)

From the womb to the tomb, these white people have "contacts" in the name of organized crime. One cop mentions, "Funeral parlors – that's something they like. They own a lot of funeral homes. They bury their own. They bury all the ones found in a trunk" (p. 297).

Let me share with you the closing passage from this chapter. It is a section of the book that deals with the "organized crime" of the future. This cop, whomever he is, does not paint a very flattering picture:

> Ten, twenty years from now, after the drug thing has run its course, the BIG thing that organized crime will get into – this is both traditional and nontraditional organized crime – will be the selling of body parts. They're already doing it in some countries – they're taking these kids, buying babies, killing them, and selling them for organ transplants. We've started to look into it here. What will happen is they'll take the babies, take the girls, take the kids, whatever ages they want, and just grow them like cattle. And then when somebody needs an organ, or a group of organs, from a three-year-old, an eight-year-old, a female white, whatever … It's really getting scientific. The fear is that the U.S. is just gonna start buying these body parts from overseas, and that's what we have to protect against, Organ farming is expected to be the next wave after drugs. Doesn't that scare you? (p. 333).

This is how the book ends: gloom peddling and posing a question instead of providing some solutions. But even with that, a manipulation was included.

The cop says that what we have to protect against is the buying of body parts from overseas. He's lying. It will be the United States that will be leading the way. What do you think cloning is all about? These white people have already violated everything else that is sacred, why not the human body? What about the prison population? Wouldn't that be a perfect source of healthy body parts? The prison population is mostly black and Latino anyway, so who cares? Death row is mostly men of color, so there is another source of body parts. There are tens of thousands of people missing every year in the United States – what do you think that is all about?

No, this country is not going to lead the way in purchasing body parts because it has plenty right here.

Plenty.

As you can see, this chapter was very informative and enlightening; not just because of the information provided regarding organized crime, but you also see the mentality behind the badge. These policemen, for the most part, are frustrated white boys with limited educational background. They live in segregated communities and hold the same views of blacks and other people of color that the white majority holds. That is what makes them so dangerous.

At the beginning of the chapter, an attempt was made to inform the reader that "organized crime" refers to any organized effort, not just the Italian version. But there should have been a follow-up, and perhaps this book is an example of that follow-up. The follow-up should be that not all "criminal" behavior is defined as such. The - should expose, to as great an extent as possible, the role that the police departments, especially big city departments – Los Angeles, Chicago, New York, Philadelphia, Detroit, Atlanta, Houston, Dallas – play in the maintenance and protection of 'organized crime." The involvement of the police, along with various members of the city government, are the key to putting the "organized" in the concept of "organized crime," are they not?

Organized Crime, Snitching and Young Rapper/Gangster Wannabes

Finally, organized crime and cops are linked to the snitch system and confidential informants. But that doesn't stop today's generation of black rappers from adopting the names of many of organized crimes biggest thugs and gangsters. The absence of black role models in the neighborhood is what I believe is the reason why so many wannabe "hip hop artists" want to use gangsters and former mobsters as their nominal social identifiers.

To begin with, one article from Ranker.com (2018) titled, "The Best Rappers Named After Gangsters," offers the following names, with my background and definition of the "original gangsters" being included. I go into detail only to show the impact that role models can have on young people and with the most recent generation, it seems that the more negative and "gangsterish" the individual, the more attractive it is to wannabe "rappers."

There's "Machine Gun Kelly", who took the name from the renowned street ganger. The real Kelly's name was George Kelly Barnes from Memphis, Tennessee and became famous during the Prohibition era. His nickname came from his favorite weapon, a Thompson submachine gun. Machine Gun Kelly spent his remaining 21 years in prison. During his time at Alcatraz he got the nickname "Pop Gun Kelly".

This was in reference, according to a former prisoner, that Kelly was a model prisoner and was nowhere near the tough, brutal gangster his wife made him out to be. He spent 17 years on Alcatraz as inmate number 117, working in the prison industries, and boasting of and exaggerating his past escapades to other inmates, and was quietly transferred back to Leavenworth in 1951. He died of a heart attack at Leavenworth on July 18, 1954, his 59th birthday (Wikipedia, 2018), and this is the man whose "name" this rapper adopted. The kid's real name is Richard Colson Baker, from Cleveland, Ohio.

Then there's "Scarface" (after Al Capone whose name was Al "Scarface" Capone). The real gangster got the nickname Capone inadvertently insulted a woman while working the door at a Brooklyn night club and was slashed by her brother Frank Gallucio. The wounds led to the nickname "Scarface" which Capone loathed.[10][11][12] When he was photographed, he hid the scarred left side of his face, saying that the injuries were war wounds.[11][13] He was called "Snorky" by his closest friends, a term for a sharp dresser (Wikipedia, 2018)

"Yo Gotti" adopted the name from original gangster John Joseph Gotti Jr. an Italian-American gangster who bee boss of the Gambino crime family in New York City. Gotti and his brothers grew up in poverty and turned to a life of crime at an early age. Gotti quickly rose to prominence, becoming one of the crime family's biggest earners and a protégé of Gambino family underboss Aniello Dellacroce, operating out of the Ozone Park neighborhood of Queens. The wannabe rapper using the gangster name is Mario Mims better known by his stage name Yo Gotti, (Wikipedia, 2018)

Then you have "Daz Dillinger," after gangster John Dillinger who wasknown for breaking out of prisons and was betrayed by "the woman in red" and brought down by Melvin Purvis. The rapper/wannabe gangster's name is Delmar Drew Arnaud (Daz Dillinger formerly Dat Nigga Daz). According to one source, he is an American rapper and record producer from Long Beach, California. Dillinger is best known for his membership of the hip hop duo Tha Dogg Pound, alongside Kurupt, as well as his work with Death Row.(Wikipedia, 2018).

And who is he imitating? None other than the gangster/thug John Herbert Dillinger, a Depression-era racketeer. Check this out, he operated with a group of men known as the Dillinger Gang or Terror Gang, which was accused of robbing 24 banks and four police stations, among other activities. Dillinger escaped from jail twice. He was also charged with, but never convicted of, the murder of an East Chicago, Indiana, police officer who shot Dillinger in his bullet-proof vest during a shootout, prompting him to return fire; despite his infamy and unlike the other members of his gang, it was Dillinger's only homicide charge.

Dillinger was hounded by Melvin Purvis, and died a horrible death after being betrayed by a "woman in red," as she was called. What she had on was the signal to the cops (she was a snitch) that the man accompanying her was Dillinger. At any rate, "Three men pursued Dillinger into the alley and fired. Clarence Hurt shot twice, Charles Winstead three times, and Herman Hollis once. Dillinger was hit from behind and fell face first to the ground ... (Wikipedia, 2018)

Dillinger was struck four times, with two bullets grazing him and one causing a superficial wound to the right side. The fatal bullet entered through the back of his neck, severed the spinal cord, passed into his brain and exited just under the right eye, severing two sets of veins and arteries.[5] An ambulance was summoned, although it was soon apparent Dillinger had died from the gunshot wounds; he was officially pronounced dead at Alexian Brothers Hospital ... According to investigators, Dillinger died without saying a word. (Wikipedia, 2018)

"Montana of 300" got the name undoubtedly from "Tony Montana" of the film version "Scarface," as portrayed by Al Pacino. The rapper's real name is Walter Anthony Bradford better known professionally as Montana of 300 (or simply Montana). Then there's Beanie Sigel" who chose the name after gangster Bugsy Siegel, known as "Bugsy". The original gangster was an American mobster and was known as one of the most "infamous and feared gangsters of his day" ...Described as handsome and charismatic, he became one of the first front-page celebrity gangsters ... He was also a driving force behind the development of the Las Vegas Strip ... Siegel was not only influential within the Jewish mob but, like his friend and fellow gangster Meyer Lansky, he also held significant influence within the American Mafia and the largely Italian-Jewish National Crime Syndicate (Wikipedia, 2018).

Beanie (born Dwight Equan Grant), on the other hand, not only "rapped" made several movies under the titled, "State Property" and "State Property II. He hails from South Philadelphia but claims that his stage name's origin is a street in South Philadelphia. Bullshit.

Tony "Scarface" Montana and the movie "Scarface" are like a cult in the black youth underground, so it is no surprise that more than one would adopt a name. This includes a rapper named "French Montana," whose birth name is Karim Kharbuoch. According to Wikipedia (2018), he was born in Morocco and immigrated to the United States with his family when he was 13. Now check out life imitating art:

> In 2003, two gunmen shot at Montana as he left a recording studio in New York, striking him in the head ... He survived and was hospitalized for several weeks ... One of the gunmen died during the incident, in what is believed to be a case of "friendly fire" by one assailant against the other. Montana was investigated

for the incident, but the case was eventually dismissed … In early 2013, Montana visited the site of the shooting with a camera crew from Life+Times as he recalled the near-death experience and his life growing up in the Bronx. This was the first time he had visited the location since the attempted murder ten years earlier … According to French, he was set up by someone close to him and his circle (Wikipedia, 2018)

There are others including "Capone-N-Noreaga," Capone-N-Noreaga (also known as C-N-N) is an American hip hop duo formed in 1995, from Queens, New York, and Irv Gotti, born Irving Domingo Lorenzo Jr., in Queens, New York. His name comes from Al Capone, of course and the other part of the duo is named after.

So what do we have in the snitch cycle? We have original gangsters, most of whom ended up dead or in prison. If they went to prison they more than likely turned some kind of state's evidence to get lesser time. Then we have another generation coming along behind them; no, not white kids, Italian, Irish or Jewish kids which is what the original gang syndicates were made of. No, this time around it's black kids and they're out there selling drugs and guns and doing what they saw their role models do in the gangster movies on television. Then when they get caught, they too become snitches, confidential informants, and agents of the state.

Another way for that to happen is to offer people who were poor and broke the law as a result, a chance to get out of it and "start all over again." That is where the Witness Protection Program comes in.

Notes on the Witness Protection Program

In my view, show me a person in the witness protection program and I'll show you a snitch. Just like Sammy the Bull: he killed 19 people and because he snitched on four Mafia families and made good on his promises as a stool pigeon, he only got give years in prison.

For better or for worse, the person "told" on someone and was now afraid to get a cap busted in his ass so the government promised him they would relocate him, give him a new identity and make sure he was never found. Only someone truly desperate would agree to never get in contact with their parents or loved ones again in life. But there's more to it than that as I will share in a minute.

According to one source,

> The United States Federal Witness Protection Program, also known as the Witness Security Program or WITSEC ... is a witness protection **program administered by the United States Department of Justice and operated by the United States Marshals Service that is designed to protect threatened witnesses before, during, and after a trial.** (Wikipedia, 2018 – emphasis added)

The witness need not have been threatened. If the system believes that the witness "might be" threatened, then that is good enough. The goal of the government is to get a conviction, and not only that, but the WITSEC also serves to isolate witnesses from their friends and families and such separation is what the system can use to take advantage of all of those left behind. Few people want to deal with this fact (more on it later).

Moving on:

> A few states, including California, Connecticut, Illinois, New York, Texas, and Washington D.C. have their own witness protection programs **for crimes not covered by the federal program.** The state-run programs **provide less extensive protections than the federal program** (Wikipedia, 2018)

The states mentioned above are the most populous states! They have the most people and therefore would have the most crime, the most kingpins, the most people who defy the government and therefore the most people who must be "snitched on" in order to bring that crime under control. Look at how pervasive the system is: "As of 2013, 8,500 witnesses and 9,900 family members have been protected by the U.S. Marshals Service since 1971 (Wikipedia, 2018).

All those people on the government dole, because the government finds the witnesses housing, pays their rents, finds them jobs, provides them with transportation and offers a monthly stipend (paycheck). More details on the witness protection program follow:

> According to Gerald Shur, the person who created the federal program, **about 95% of witnesses in the program are "criminals".** They may be intentional criminals, or people who are doing business with criminals, such as one engineer who bought off a mayor "because that's how you do business in the city. In his mind, he wasn't doing anything criminal", as Shur said. **A witness who agrees to testify for the prosecution is generally eligible to join the program, which is entirely voluntary.** Witnesses are permitted to leave the program and

> return to their original identities at any time, **although this is always discouraged by administrators** (Wikipedia, 2018 – emphasis added)

I would go so far to say that ninety-five percent of witnesses in the program HAVE BEEN CONVINCED that they have violated the law in some way. The fear of having done that and the thought of being butt-raped in prison is the deterrence. So these people "cop a plea" and "beg" for something or someone that they can hand over. That is how they are offered a chance to get into the witness protection program.

More background is in order:

> The WITSEC program was formally established under Title V of the Organized Crime Control Act of 1970, which in turn sets out the manner in which the United States Attorney General may provide for the relocation and protection of a witness or potential witness of the federal or state government in an official proceeding concerning organized crime or other serious offenses. See 18 U.S.C.A 3521, *et. seq.* The federal government also gives grants to the states to enable them to provide similar services. (Wikipedia, 2018)

Established in 1970 – during the height of the social turmoil that was tearing the country apart. The Black Panther Party was at its zenith, as were the Nation of Islam, the Revolutionary Action Movement, the Weathermen, the Students for a Democratic Society, the Red Guard, the Brown Beret, and other groups that were rebelling against America's racist, imperialistic and misogynistic ways.

That was when the snitches were given form and function. Captured would-be revolutionaries snatched of the streets, "tuned up" by cops, intimidated, placed in cells with huge men who rape them, and then intimidated into doing the bidding of the system. From that point the numbers began to increase. One such snitch is quoted extensively in this book. Others were plucked from the ranks of the military and some were just "good ol' niggers" who wanted to get into the FBI, so snitching and infiltrating black groups was a kind of 'initiation.'

But go back ten years from 1970s:

> WITSEC was originally created as the Federal Witness Protection Program in the mid-1960s by Gerald Shur, when he was Attorney in Charge of the Intelligence and Special Services Unit of the Organized Crime and Racketeering Section of the United States Department of Justice … **Most witnesses are**

> **protected by the United States Marshals Service, while protection of incarcerated witnesses is the duty of the Federal Bureau of Prisons.** (Wikipedia, 2018 – emphasis added)

Those who agree to snitch are "protected." John F. Kennedy wasn't protected (Dallas, TX., November 1963); Malcolm X wasn't protected (New York, 1965); Martin Luther King, Jr,. wasn't protected (Memphis, Tennessee, April 1968). Robert F. Kennedy wasn't protected (Los Angeles, 1968); Meir Kahana wasn't protected (New York, 1990). But if you sell your soul to indict someone who has pissed off the system one way or another, then you get protection by either the United States Marshal's Service or the Federal Bureau of Prisons.

> Former decorated federal law enforcement officer John Thomas Ambrose was convicted of leaking information about a federal witness in the Witness Protection Program, Chicago Outfit hitman Nicholas Calabrese, to other members of Chicago organized crime (Wikipedia, 2018)

We have to bear in mind that "A witness who agrees to testify for the prosecution is generally eligible to join the program, which is entirely voluntary." That is not true. The witness protection program may appear to be voluntary, but the fact is a great deal of coercion and manipulation are involved that lead the witness to come to the conclusion that the witness protection program is his/her best option. How else to convince someone that they will never see family members again, must surrender all their personal items, adopt a new identity and move to an entirely different city or town. That person may not be guilty of a crime, but the government has certainly convinced him/her that their life is threatened and that the program is their best option and outlet

Note the nebulous claim that the person can return to his or her own identity at any time, "although this is always discouraged by administrators." Just like entry into the program is "voluntary." These peckerwoods manipulate the entire situation. Once you enter the program that means you learn the government's secrets. Once that is done, why would they allow you to return the regular civilian life and spill your guts? Sure, it has been done, but that comes at the risk of the person who was the witness and long after the defendants have been locked up or put to death.

According to one source,

> In both criminal and civil matters involving protected witnesses, the U.S. Marshals **cooperate fully with local law enforcement**

and court authorities to bring witnesses to justice or to have them fulfill their legal responsibilities (Wikipedia, 2018 – emphasis added)

So the local cops know who these snitches are. And this is what is taking place in Omaha, one of the key cities where people in the witness protection program are placed. Later in this book I discuss the "snitch system" in Omaha as it relates to black youth and as one of the many causes of black-on-black youth crime that intermittently takes place within the boundaries of a segregated black community that is only eight square miles in circumference yet holds more than 80% of the city's African-Americans.

Check out the following tidbit of information:

> Less than 17 percent of protected witnesses who have committed a crime **will be caught committing another crime**, compared to the almost 41 percent of parolees who return to crime (Wikipedia, 2018 – emphasis added)

What difference does this make? Why wouldn't someone who is given government protection not feel that he or she is "above the law" and then move on to commit another crime?

Notes on the "Confidential Informant"

Next, let us discuss the "confidential informant."

> An **informant** (also called an **informer**) … is a person who provides **privileged information about a person or organization to an agency.** The term is usually used within the law enforcement world, where they are officially known as **confidential** or **criminal informants (CI)**, and can often refer pejoratively to the supply of information without the consent of the other parties with the intent of malicious, personal or financial gain … However, the term is used in politics, industry and academia (Levine, 2009 – emphasis added)

The old folks always taught us that "what is done in the dark will soon come to the light." White people are masters of deception and cowardly activity. They are equally adept at making behind-closed-doors decisions, formulating a plan, and then coming out in public with a united front.

The confidential informant is a coward, no matter how you slice it. I say this because if you are defending the American system or any of its components, you are defending a system and a people with a long history of criminality. America is no cradle of morality and one need only look at the election of 2016 and since that time to see these white people beginning to see the buffoonery and evil in their system that we, as Black people, have witnessed and been victims of for the past 350 years.

Having said that, here is what Levine (2009) has to say about the use of the confidential informant:

> Informants are **commonly found in the world of organized crime.** By its very nature, organized crime involves many people who are aware of each other's guilt, in a variety of illegal activities. Quite frequently, confidential informants (or criminal informants) will provide information **in order to obtain lenient treatment for themselves and provide information, over an extended period of time, in return for money or for police to overlook their own criminal activities.** Quite often, someone will become an informant **following their arrest** (Levine, 2009 – e emphasis added)

All crime in America is "organized" on some level, even if it's just a pickpocket. What is meant above is aimed at ethnic groups: Italians, the Irish, the Russians, the black gangs and so on. The REAL organized crime is taking place in Washington, DC in the halls of Congress and in the House of Representatives. That is where the trickledown effect of "evil" begins and the Mafia and related groups are just the recipients of the criminal crumbs handed down by those old white boys who wear the same color suit and ties every single day.

You will hear these people talk about the immigrants and how "this is a nation of immigrants." It sure is. Every immigrant group that came over here got involved in organized crime. The early immigrants were scum of the earth, sent here as a penalty for murder, rape, theft and so on. The same was done to the penal colony of Australia. White people have always been criminals and they brought it to these shores and set out to re-establish it in their colonies – after murdering off the First Nation people that is.

So the concept of "justice" is a philosophical one, not a moral one. Why would criminals and the descendants of criminals give a damn about justice? The most money is made in America when the rules are bent or twisted or violated outright. The farmer steals and lies on his reports, the corporations falsify their tax forms, the employer hires people "off the books", and the schools lie and claim that they are actually "educating" young people. In return the cities, counties and states receive free money (known as "grants") that they then use to continue their organized criminality.

By their own admission, you have to have a crime on your record to be of value as a confidential informant. Once you've screwed up and gotten caught, that is when they have you. And that is why, "Informants are also extremely common in every-day police work, including homicide and narcotics investigations. Any citizen who provides crime related information to law enforcement by definition is an informant" (Levine, 2009) And that's on your record and can be used against you whenever they want to.

According to one article,

> The CIA has been criticized for leniency towards drug lords and murderers acting as paid informants, informants being allowed to engage in some crimes so that the potential informant can blend into the criminal environment without suspicion ... and wasting billions of dollars on dishonest sources of information (Levine, 2009)

Check out the terminology: "Dishonest sources of information." Is this in reference to the person as the source or the information as the source? How about the situation being the source of disinformation, meaning law enforcement being so desperate to "do the right thing" that they wrangle information out of criminals who snitch on other criminals and in this case, "two wrongs make a right." As long as these peckerwoods get a conviction, that's all they seem to care about. To them, "the ends justifies the means."

According to one source,

> Informants are often regarded as traitors by their former criminal associates. **Whatever the nature of a group, it is likely to feel strong hostility toward any known informers, regard them as threats and inflict punishments ranging from social ostracism through physical abuse and/or death**. Informers are therefore generally protected, either by being **segregated while in prison** or, if they are not incarcerated, **relocated under a new identity** (Levine, 2009 emphasis added)

The hostility that is felt is not just against the snitch and what he/she has done by 'telling'; it is against the system itself because of its desperation tactic to drag in a "third party" in order to "get" the "bad guys." If the bad guys are slick enough to get away from the government and the government so goony and buffoon-like that it can't get the job done, why drag in some snitch and offer them some trinkets in exchange for what I view as "tainted testimony"? Yet other sources claim,

> Informants, and especially criminal informants, can be motivated by many reasons. **Many informants are not themselves aware of all of their reasons for providing information, but nonetheless do so.** Many informants provide information **while under stress, duress, emotion and other life factors that can impact the accuracy or veracity of information provided**. Law enforcement officers, prosecutors, defense lawyers, judges and others **should be aware of possible motivations so that they can properly approach, assess and verify informants' information**. (Johnson, 1961; Levine, 2009 – emphasis added)

The previous quote, a combination of information from two "scholars" is pure bullshit. These white people want to make it appear as if there are some snitches who don't know why they are snitching. Ain't that a bitch? Of course they know why: they want to save their own ass! Literally! That means staying out of prison and getting screwed up the butt by some huge inmate or waking up with a big black penis waving at you! That fear is enough to make someone tell on their own mama!

Furthermore, the purpose of the "snitch" is to put someone else in a position where the snitch fears to be. So he (or she) simply "tells." The only stress takes place when the Feds find out that someone is telling a lie and leading them on a wild goose chase.

According to Wikipedia (2018), informants turn to snitching because of one of three motivations: (1) self-interest, (2) self-preservation, or (3) conscience.

In terms of self interest there is financial reward, you can receive a pre-trial release from custody (but sometimes this can backfire because people who are watching are going to wonder what you did to receive such a "break", you can have your charges withdrawn or dismissed in exchange for telling on someone else, you can get a reduction in your own sentence, you can tell on your competitor gangsters and get them off the streets, you can divert attention away from your own crimes and of course, there is always the "payback" factor – getting revenge similar to what Sammy Gravano did to his criminal pals.

Self-preservation is another reason that people snitch, tattle, or "talk." They do it because they are afraid of being harmed by others, they may have been threatened with other charges or threatened with more jail time or they actually have a desire to enter the witness protection program.

Finally, there is "conscience." You snitch because you have a desire to do the right thing or "go straight," you tell because for whatever reason, you may have a guilty conscience. And then there are the do-gooders who have a desire to help the cops and society (yeah, right!).

SNITCH: A LONGITUDINAL STUDY

Throughout history there have been those who have betrayed their own particular group; Benedict Arnold, Vidkun Quisling and more recently, the Rosenbergs and Bernie Madoff come to mind. But even in popular culture, there were names made used in the movies by the likes of Humphrey Bogart, Jimmy Cagney and others for a person who collaborated with the police. Names like "canary," "fink," "rat," "snitcher," "stool pigeon" and "stoolie" come to mind

A "snitch" is defined as, "someone acting as an informer or decoy for the police." Omaha has long had sellouts and those who would betray the black community. In my own journalistic quest to address the present-day spate of police informants, many of them juveniles who are "dropping dimes" on each other in an attempt to get less time for drug charges, I found that indeed, the concept of "telling" was something that young people are not afraid to do. In act, many of them have a philosophy that, "There's two kinds of people: those who told and those who wish they had told." This mentality or philosophy prompted me to ask myself the question: "where did these kids get the idea that "telling" was something to be proud of?

In October of 2004 it was reported that, **the State of Nebraska, as backward and rural as it is, ranks number one in the nation in the most Federal drug cases lodged in its courts.** How could a state so backward in so many respects rank so high in terms of drugs unless the cops were buffoons? Unless the cops, to cancel out their ineptitude, had a complex snitch system? Unless Omaha, the biggest city, was doing the most plotting, the most manipulating, the most arresting and convicting of residents – mainly youth of color?

My research uncovered some key facts regarding a number of incidents or situations where it is clear that "telling" or "snitching" was a key component of the betrayal of the black community. In this brief essay, I document eight of them.

1938 – The Omaha Star and its Anti-Snitch/Anti-Sellout Message

At the root of much of the betrayal that some inflict upon our community is the reality that there is a great deal of concern about and commitment to developing our community as well as defending it against those who would do it harm. Sometimes that harm comes from the outside; many times it is inflicted from within.

For example, on July 30, 1938, the question posed by "The Roving Reporter," a regular feature in the *Omaha Star*, was "What is needed most by the Negro of Omaha?" Mr. Floyd Buckner of 2226 Miami Street answered, "A real leader, an upright Christian person, someone who lives a clean life. Because politics is running the Negro of Omaha." Mr. Robert I. Britt of 2922 North 25th Street and an employee of Union Pacific, said,

> "What is most needed by the Negro of Omaha is a liberal minded and civic and political organization to band, stick and fight together under group leadership in order to obtain the political, economic and civic proportion which the group rightfully merits. It is a plain fact that the men of the community are lax in these things. It is with regret that I state that the women show more initiative in the upbuilding of times and principle in this community, than the men."

The same edition of the paper posed the question to Mr. W.L. Seals of 2808 Binney Street, a government employee, who said, "One of the greatest things needed by Negro of Omaha is the re-establishment of confidence. The breaking down of class distinction and clanishment, and to be ever mindful that we are our brother's keeper, to think more helping and less of knocking one another."

These questions clearly show that our predecessors were progressive-thinking in spite of the segregation that permeated the city and the racism that was the foundation of race relations. Little has changed since then, so the question is: where is the "roving reporter" of today? Can we expect the Omaha World Herald to ask the tough questions? Of course not. Can we expect the Omaha Star to do it? Perhaps – with a little prodding. More on that later.

On August 13, 1938 edition of the Omaha Star, the following editorial titled, "The Omaha Star is Here to Stay," appeared to be more prophetic than many could have realized at that time. Following is the editorial in its entirety:

> The Omaha Star began six weeks ago. To be exact, the first edition hit the streets on July 9. On that day, it was dedicated to the service of the people that no good cause shall lack a champion and that evil shall not thrive unopposed.
>
> As we give you the sixth edition of the most progressive Negro weekly in the middle west, we are glad to state to thousands of true Americans, who have learned to admire the Omaha Star for its straight from the shoulder editorials and its feature of local news augmented with well written and interesting columns, that it is here to stay!
>
> This statement is being made in light of propaganda that is being spread ***by some unscrupulous individual or individuals to the effect that the Omaha Star is a political paper and that its life will terminate following the general election on November 9.***
>
> In regards to politics and the Omaha Star, may it be known that the Star has the intestinal fortitude to take a stand, based upon its own conviction. And that stand will unerringly be magnified through its editorials.
>
> The Star will at no time be found upon the fence or allow itself to be branded a double-crosser. It is the servant of the people and as such it will operate.
>
> The spirit of *the new Negro* will be exemplified through the Star, a spirit that is definitely driving for the freedom of the Negro from economic bondage, a condition which if allowed to continue will ultimately return 15,000,000 souls back to chattel slavery. This is a battle that every true American must join. Stoop not to false propaganda. Know where of you speak and above all speak the truth.
>
> The Star, a paper who just last week placed money into the pockets of many of our youth and seven adults is deserving of your support and not your knocks.
>
> **Listen not to those vicious, serpent-like individuals who seek to prevent a legitimate business from progressing through unwarranted propaganda.** Give the Omaha Star a firm foundation by way of subscribing and reading support and we will assure you that we in turn will build an enterprise worthy of consideration, mouthpiece and a force for the people. The Omaha Star is here to stay! (emphasis added

Bold words from a bold organization with a bold mission. But from that excerpt, two things are clear. First, that there were people who felt that following an election, the Star would disappear. Secondly, that there are people who wanted to spread rumors that they hoped would hurt the fledgling newspaper. It is these kinds of people from whom the Uncle Tom and sellout – the "snitch" – can be extracted. They have always been among our ranks. But they are at their most audacious today in the year 2004.

<u>1959: The Beginning of COINTELPRO</u>

Before we get into the turbulent 60's and the like, let's go to the '60s, Martin Luther King, Jr., and the snitch that he had sitting right up under him during his speeches and protests. Wold (2015) writes,

> **Beginning in 1956, the FBI launched the mother of all snitching operations known as COINTELPRO, an abbreviation of Counterintelligence Program**. But this wasn't the usual counterintelligence program. Instead of spying on foreign governments, **this program targeted American citizens**. With COINTELPRO, **the FBI attempted to disrupt and splinter the American left, targeting any and every group advocating progressive change**. Part of the FBI's stated mission for COINTELPRO was **"maintaining the existing social and political order."** (Wold, 2015 – emphasis added)

And since the existing and political order is a lily-white and racist one, then this was the unspoken (though overriding) vision of this program. It was the same one that would be used a decade later against the Black Panther Party for Self-Defense, the Weathermen, the Students for a Democratic Society, the Brown Beret, the Red Guard, the Republic of New Africa, the Nation of Islam and many others. The white government of the United States was afraid of communism, but more importantly it was afraid of – nigguz!

And that "the immigrants are invading and coming this way" scare that President Donald Trump used just before the 2018 midterm elections was already in place. Only the immigrants were domestic people of color who were protesting, burning and picketing against a racist government.

So it's probably not a coincidence that the system for snitching was set up only two years after the passage of the Brown v. Board decision that made it illegal to segregate public facilities. But when the white history writers give a date for the "beginning" of any government plan or program, this means that the program has been in the planning stages for at least two years prior to that.

Snitches and confidential informants became "soldiers" in this white racist government's attacks on people of color. As Wold (2015) wrote,

> Snitches with COINTELPRO surveilled, infiltrated, and exposed the secrets of a variety of progressive groups including protesters of the Vietnam War, civil rights organizations, a Native American advocacy group, the Black Panthers, and activist groups in the women's rights movement.

But as we know, when the white liberal has a cold, black folks have got pneumonia. So if a white system as going after its own race members over differences in viewpoint, you KNOW what they were going to do in the case of those who had different cultural backgrounds and skin color. They not only infiltrated and spied, but also told lies that went into reports that would be used in a court of law to 'set up" those who were deemed "radicals" or "militants."

The next excerpt is filled with conjecture but the general nature of the point is well-made as follows:

> Perhaps the best known COINTELPRO target **was civil rights icon Dr. Martin Luther King Jr.** Accordingly, the FBI secured a snitch with access to King **who also happened to be one of the most prominent photographers documenting the civil rights movement.** Ernest Withers was a trusted confidant of Martin Luther King Jr. **He photographed some of the most important moments in King's life**. (Wold, 2015 – emphasis added)

Those of us in the black nationalist movement who study and do our own research know that King was "busted" almost right away. First of all, he loved white women and got caught screwing more than a few of them. After all, Ralph Abernathy, Andrew Young and a few other "leaders" had his back, so he knew he could get away with it. Even when the FBI taped him having sex with a couple of women and sent the tapes to his wife, Coretta, that didn't stop King from fraternizing.

Secondly, King was engaged to marry a white woman before he even met Coretta. But his mentor talked him out of it telling him that the ministers in Georgia had a special mission in mind for him and marrying a white woman would not be wise. So these men introduced him to the light-skinned Coretta Scott, who King would eventually marry. All of this is on tape, from the hounding before marriage to the sex during the marriage with women other than his wife.

But my disagreement with the excerpt by Wold is his claim that King was the best known of the COINTELPRO targets. I beg to differ. He might have been the most prominent of the "civil rights" leaders, but American history is quick to omit the power, influence and vision of those who were involved in the Black Power movement. It was this movement that talked about changing (not necessarily integrating into) the system and about race and about the white man's heinous history. And that is the movement that the system feared and hated the most.

With that in mind, the most prominent would have to have been Huey P. Newton and members of the Black Panther Party. They were all over the nation with branches in cities from west to east, while King was mostly a "southern" concern. In addition to the Black Panther Party there was Karenga and US (who many say was a snitch himself), there was the Revolutionary Action Movement, the Republic of New Africa and its leader Imari Abubakari Obadele, the many other groups along with campuses filled with militant Black Student Unions. No matter who you choose, everyone got snitched on and every group got infiltrated.

One researcher writes that,

> **All the while, though, he was receiving paychecks from the FBI for the photographs he sent them, which were used to anticipate his every move, disrupt his protests, and even blackmail him.** Withers also provided the FBI with information about other activists, pastors, **and candidates running for public office.** He told the FBI of planned civil rights demonstrations **so the FBI could try to disrupt the protests**. (Wold, 2015 – emphasis added)

This is the REAL FBI! All these kudos and compliments being showered on Robert Mueller and the investigation of President Donald Trump is Johnny-come-lately bullshit and revisionist history. Give it a name! The FBI has done more dirt or as much dirt as organized crime, and they did it against legitimate organizations, haunting and hunting them simply because they had skin color. And that is what made these snitches all that money and kept those black pastors quiet in that pulpit. They talked that bullshit on Sunday, but many of them had been caught in some shady situations and were under the control of the local and the federal versions of the FBI – just like that Dr. King's photographer.

> The FBI used some of this information to break into one of King's hotel rooms and recorded evidence of an extramarital affair. Afterward, they sent a letter to King directly, claiming they would blackmail him and implying they would leak the information if he didn't commit suicide in the next 34 days. The FBI told King, "You are done. There is but one way out for you. You better take it before your filthy, abnormal fraudulent self is bared to the nation." (Wold, 2015).

More revisionist history. King was caught on more than one occasion and not all of them were recorded. The information about getting him to commit suicide sounds shakey because then he would have evidence to use that would "counter" the FBI's attempted sting. But be that as it may, this is a man going around talking about God, about morality, about a crisis of conscience and all the time he was screwing around behind his wife's back. Others would follow shit in subsequent years, including the Urban League's Vernon Jordan, Dr. King's protégé's Jesse Jackson and Andrew Young, and many others we haven't heard about.

1960 - COINTELPRO: Snitches, Confidential Informants and Sellouts

Wold (2015) writes about the Black Panther Party for Self-Defense, which was started in the Fall of 1966 and moved on almost as quickly:

> Another FBI snitch with the COINTELPRO program was in the Black Panther Party and supplied the FBI with a floor plan of the building where Black Panther leader Fred Hampton was staying. **The floor plan was used in an FBI raid in which Hampton was assassinated by the FBI and Chicago Police Department**. (Wold, 2015 – emphasis added)

Legalized assassinations taking place right here in America, in full view of the public and the media, and the only thing that people would say was "too bad." Black men who were fighting for the right to defend themselves and their communities being gunned down in their sleep. I spoke with Fred's wife back in 1992 during a "Call to Arms Summit" organized by then Milwaukee Black Panther Militia leader Michael McGee. She described the entire scenario and described how the invading cops riddled the doors with so many bullets that if you just touched it the door would have disintegrated.

The FBI working in conjunction and cahoots with the local police department. All of this was based on race and racism and the snitches made the already over-armed cops' jobs that much easier. How did we find out about COINTELPRO and what it was doing. According to Wold (2015), "COINTELPRO only came to light when a group of activists broke into the FBI's offices in 1971 and stole documents detailing the program. **Soon after, the program was terminated by FBI director J. Edgar Hoover.**" (emphasis added)

The last part of the previous quote is bullshit. COINTELPRO was not terminated in 1971. Those of us in the movement know this to be a lie and we know that just because you might change the name of a program or project doesn't mean that the "mission" doesn't still continue. One source provided a wealth of additional information:

> While COINTELPRO was officially terminated in April 1971, domestic espionage continued.[91][92][93] Between 1972 and 1974, it is documented that the Bureau planted over 500 bugs without a warrant and opened over 2,000 pieces of personal mail. More recent targets of covert action include the American Indian Movement (AIM), Earth First!, and Committees in Solidarity with the People of El Salvador.[94] ... "Counterterrorism" guidelines implemented during the Reagan administration have been described as allowing a return to COINTELPRO tactics ... COINTELPRO survivor Filiberto Ojeda Rios was killed by the FBI's hostage rescue team in 2005 ... his death described as an assassination by a United Nations special committee (Wikipedia, 2018)

In my view COINTELPRO exists even today into 2018. While the major networks are singing the praises of the FBI because of its work with the Russian cyber attacks on the 2016 election. Most seem to have forgotten the murders of black civilians by this same organization, with the blessing of the U.S. government.

Snitches even wrote books about what they did. One was published in 1973 under the title, The Glass House Tapes - The Story of an Agent Provocateur and the New Police Intelligence Complex by Louis E. Tackwood and was circulated throughout the black nationalist community. But another one (actually two) was shared with the public regarding the exploits of one Earl Anthony. The books were *Picking up the Gun: A Report on the Black Panthers* (1970) and *Spitting Against the Wind: The True Story Behind the Violent Legacy of the Black Panther Party* (1990).

Government Snitch: Earl Anthony and His Antics

Earl Anthony came to discuss the event at an early November 1967 meeting of the Black Congress Executive Committee. He wore the Black Panther uniform: black leather jacket, black pants, powder-blue shirt. He told us he was on the Central Committee of the Black Panther Party for Self-Defense. Like the rest of the black militant organizations, the Black Panthers had come into being only in the last year or so. Unlike the rest, they had drawn their guns. They walked the streets of Oakland openly armed, to challenge any police who were assaulting blacks." (Brown, p. 113).

Please keep in mind that Earl Anthony was a snitch, and he seemingly just walked into the ranks of the Black Panther Party. He describes his experiences in both of his books, *Picking Up the Gun: A Report on the Black Panther Party* (1970) and then twenty years later published, *Spitting in the Wind: The True Story Behind the Violent Legacy of the Black Panther Party* (1990). This muthafucka not only infiltrated the Party and rose up in the ranks, but he got mo pussy than Iceberg Slim during the time he was there (he got kicked out in 1979).

As an FBI informant Anthony's mere presence in the Party showed how weak and undisciplined the organization was. Here is what Elaine Brown writes in her book:

> "Brothers, this is an emergency," Anthony announced.
> "Last month, Brother Huey P. Newton, minister of defense
> of the Black Panther Party for Self-Defense, was taken
> hostage by the pig. He was seized off the streets of
> Oakland after an armed agent of the Man was shot and
> killed in a righteous at of self defense. One of the pigs was
> killed when they tried to kill Huey. Yeah, Brothers, it was
> a 'red-light trial,' a trial by fire on the streets of Babylon.
> Brother Huey took care of business. Now he is the political
> prisoner of our enemy. I'm here to get you Brothers ...
> Karenga interrupted ... (Brown, pp. 113-114)

Who was this muthafucka? According to Elaine a Panther officer named Walter Bremond had brought Earl Anthony to the meeting. I think I remember this muthafucka, having seen pictures of him many years later. He was always visible, talking loud and making himself seen. Now I know why. I read his book, Picking Up the Gun many years later and now, in retrospect, we all know he was a government agent. And, as you can see in the previous excerpt, he had the dress and the Panther rhetoric down pat.

In fact, Anthony was the eighth member to join the Black Panther Party. He was a part of the group that picked Betty Shabazz up at the airport and served as her bodyguards. Just think: an FBI agent in the ranks guarding the widow of Malcolm X. Betty could have been hurt or killed because these "Panthers" didn't have enough sense or concern to screen those they were allowing into their membership. This is more evidence that these niggas were nothing more than a street gang on steroids. Nothing more, nothing less.

Perhaps it was just a matter of physical appearance. But I personally blame that sick fuck Eldridge Cleaver. Anthony claims that it was Cleaver who made the initial introductions:

> When I returned later, Cleaver was there. He introduced me to five or six Panthers -- the entire membership with the exception of Huey Newton, who was nowhere about. Then the two of us went into another room and talked. He seemed interested in my desire to join the Panthers but cautious. Up until that point all the membership, with the exception of Eldridge, were home boys from the Oakland area. (Anthony, 1990: 25)

And perhaps that is the way it should have stayed, because Cleaver -- like Anthony -- would play major roles in the internal problems that the Party would have later down the road. Like takes to like: Cleaver was an abuser, an idiot and a megalomaniac and yet he was referred to by Panther leadership as their "best writer."

At that same meeting Sis. Elaine Brown, of all people, stood up for the brother and asked that Anthony be allowed to continue to speak. They -- Elaine and Bremond -- were voted down, and Anthony never got a chance to finish explaining. But Elaine wrote in her book, "I was charmed by the Black Panther stuff; Earl Anthony had style, I thought." (Brown, p. 114). See how this bitch is: she's just as dick hungry as the regular street sister, and probably has less moral fortitude. She talks all that Black Panther shit but when you read this analysis you will see that she's all talk: like the misogynistic and megalomaniac-oriented black men, she represents the worse in black female identity.

From there Earl began attending the weekly Black Congress meetings,

> ... though he never petitioned the Congress to include the Oakland Panthers in its membership. Perhaps it had to do with the technicality that Earl represented only the Huey Newton Legal Defense Fund, which was organized around a limited agenda, unlike the NAACP and other organizations which had representatives in the Congress. Nevertheless, Earl was coming every week to report on the progress of the Huey Newton Legal Defense Fund and, afterward, inviting me to ride with him (Brown, pp. 114-115).

So not only did Elaine trust (and fuck) this snitch, but so did Eldridge Cleaver and a host of other people who should have known better. There were no checks and balances, no screening process, whatsoever. Had I known this I probably could have walked in and joined in 1971 when Barney and I were hitch hiking from Pittsburg to Oakland and sitting outside for hours on end watching these assholes march in and out of the headquarters.

So this FBI mole is having his way (literally and figuratively speaking) with the Panthers on all levels. He's snitching, he's lecturing, he's fuckin', he's just having a damn ball. And Elaine can talk shit in retrospect but, like Cleaver, she was partially responsible for Anthony's access to any information he was able to obtain. In her own words:

> I became Earl's entourage of one. I would accompany him after the Congress meetings to gatherings of black professionals or college students or neighborhood groups, whom he would call upon to "join the struggle," to support Huey Newton. Earl also invited me to his bed. I wondered, later, what made me accept Earl's nagging invitation ...
> (Brown, p. 115).

Look at this bitch trying to play dumb and naïve. She wonders what made her accept his invitation. I'll tell you why: because she's a whore, that's why! Elaine Brown was easy pussy for anybody who had a rap, who had some semblance of "juice" and who showed an interest in her. Elsewhere in this book you saw where she and a girlfriend were debating over who would fuck Eldridge Cleaver, and that was one ugly muthafucka! But he had fame and notoriety and that's all bitches like Elaine Brown are concerned about. She's a slut and she's weak-minded as well. For instance, read the following:

> Perhaps I thought of it as having to do with the freedom of black people. Earl had suggested such a thing. He had actually told me that a true Sister would be happy to sleep with a revolutionary Brother. Obviously, revolutionariness was not close to cleanliness, I thought as I entered Earl's unkempt house. One night with him was enough ... (p. 115)

So he was nasty and she fucked him anyway. But more importantly, what she just wrote is not quite the way Anthony tells it in his book. He refers to her at one point as, "Elaine Brown, my former girlfriend and now a Panther leader." (Anthony, p. 151) This tends to mean that he fucked her more than once. And, he further claims, "Back in 1968, Brown had come around to the home of my parents in Los Angeles, trying to find my whereabouts. That was when the Panthers had a contract out on my life ..." (Anthony, p. 151). So what she tries to make sound like a mercy fuck turns out to be her chasing after this guy regardless of how unclean she claimed his house would.

The question we must ask ourselves therefore, is why would Elaine be looking for Anthony if she despised him so much? Why would she write in her autobiography, *A Taste of Power*, that,

> It was hard to believe Earl Anthony had found the nerve to call me again. I had made it clear to him months ago that he disgusted me, at best. He was still in Southern California, still working for the Huey Newton Legal Defense Fund and now also working with Bunchy Carter. He was writing press statements and pamphlets for the new Southern California chapter, he told me, as though I had an interest in him. He was also telling me something about attending a rally for Huey Newton's birthday. It was a political rally to raise funds and consciousness in connection with the pending trial of Huey Newton for the killing of the white Oakland cop back in October. (pp. 125-126).

That lying bitch. She should have called the book, "A Taste of Sperm" because it seems that she sucked more dick that Monica Lewinsky! She makes herself sound irresistible and sought after when, in reality, she was the one who was doing the pursuing. And the reason why I believe Anthony's account is because this is the bitch who was introducing him around and she held Cleaver in high esteem. And Anthony had Cleaver's stamp of approval as well.

So this section was titled, "Snitches, Confidential Informants and Sell-Outs" for a reason. In most cases those who snitch and those who serve as confidential informants get paid. But it is the sellout who is the dog muthafucka who just betrays people for the sake of doing it. And I think that Elaine Brown, as courageous and audacious as she is on the one hand, is still a stupid bitch who made major mistakes on the other hand, and these mistakes are of the type that made it possible for the snitches and confidential informants to gain a foothold in the Party from the very outset.

If beating on women, violating what few rules there apparently were, and outright lying weren't bad enough, let's take a look at interracial sex (which I refer to as "miscegenation" which is an antiquated term, but effective) and the role that it played in what I view as the "demise" not only of the Black Panther Party, but as I hope to show, the eventual undermining and destruction of the entire black liberation movement.

Let me state right here that I am old school, but I've had a lot of women and anyone who knows me knows that. And from my many years of experience, as a black man, I know about two stigmas that most of us avoid: (1) we don't like the idea of buying pussy from prostitutes. Now since I think that most housewives are prostitutes anyway, I also know that they sell pussy in a legally accepted way and I deal with this in my other publications. (2) black men don't eat pussy. Those who do keep it quiet and personally, I only performed it with my wife or with women I had deep feelings for, and that was very few. Black men consider it an insult and during insults you might hear one call another, "You pussy eatin' muthafucka." In some cases, those are fighting words.

The point made here is that this man, Earl Anthony, thinks and acts like a white man. His hatred of women in general and black women in particular, is reflected in his writings, which I have documented and analyzed on the following pages of this chapter. I don't really give a shit about Earl Anthony except for an important point: he played a major role in infiltrating the Panthers, spreading rumors and the like, led to the deaths of a lot of well-meaning bruthas.

Earl Anthony was a race traitor who sold us all out to the white man, a cross-dressing asshole by the name of J. Edgar Hoover. Then he bragged about it and wrote about it. His writings degraded black and white women and in many cases used their actual names and the cities that they lived in as he painted them all to look like nothing more than his willing thralls.

For these reasons and others that I will provide, we have enough motivation to expose this sonofabitch. But as you will see there are other reasons. And maybe if you took your finger out of your ass long enough and cracked a fuckin' book, you'd know what I know. But at any rate, with my central concerns provided, let's look at the issues of Earl Anthony, the men of the Black Panther Party, the hatred of women and the role that interracial relationships (black men fucking white women) played in the demise of the black liberation movement in general and the Black Panther Party, in particular.

Secondly, let me just say here and now that I have met a few people during my life that I would consider totally without worth. Not many, but a few. There is no doubt in my mind that after all the reading I have done on the Panthers and black leadership, that when it comes to mind numbing worthlessness as a human being, the FBI snitch Earl Anthony reigns without rivtal. I will show you how I arrived at this conclusion on the pages that follow in this chapter.

Elaine Brown was fortunate because the informant, Earl Anthony, in addition to being an informant, was also a woman-beater. And the Panther men like Anthony – and not unlike so many black men in our communities -- seemed to be fascinated with white women. In fact, Anthony boasts about it throughout his book, *Spitting in the Wind.* Following are excerpts which also prove he was a quasi-rapist.

For instance, here is how he got the white women he dated to give up sex after they said no or were hesitant:

> "I was to stay there until November. I stayed with a young Anglo woman named June and worked as a public relations director for an African dramatic company." (Anthony, p. 66).

Do you see what I see? This is the 1960s and the "black and proud" environment has enveloped the Bay Area. But one thing is present in almost all quarters: the white woman. Whether it's Jean Seberg and Jane Fonda donating money and screwing bruthas on the side, or in this case, the young white girl who is allowing Earl Anthony to stay with her at her home/apartment, the fact still remains: black men have been lynched, castrated and murdered for centuries over this bitch but, for some reason, we can't seem to get her out of the equation and, even worse, we don't seem to want to.

Sleeping white while talking black persists to this day locally here in Omaha and on a national basis and while it may not necessarily be black politicians, those black men with visibility and money certainly seem prone:

from Sidney Portier, Sammy Davis, Jr., Quincy Jones and Michael Jackson back in the day to Kanye West, Lamar Odom, Clarence Thomas, Tiki Barber and Lamar Odom today. Black women don't like it but many have accepted it, but they accept it as evidence of the stereotypical belief that, for the most part, "black men ain't shit."

Earl Anthony, the snitch, continues:

> "That night I went to see blues singer Joe Williams at a nightclub. I met a hippie white chick at the club, bought her drinks, then we went to her commune, which was crowded with her commune buddies -- male and female. We talked then found an empty room and had sex." (Anthony, p. 83).

This coon goes to a nightclub to see blues singer Joe Williams, one of the greats. And of all the black women who must have been there he singles out what he calls a "hippie white chick" and then goes into one of those nasty ass commune settings (according to Elaine he was nasty himself) and fucked her. So the FBI chose wisely when they got this guy to work for them because his "perks" – white bitches – were enough to ensure that he would be a snitch with a long shelf life. Continuing:

> "That night Hobbs and I had dinner. It was then that he told me that he and Haskins were into white women. I didn't believe it at first because Hobbs' office was staffed fully by black women -- all high yellow -- like my soon-to-be wife, Robin Bruce, who was his receptionist. Hobbs asked me if I'd like to hang out with him and Haskins. I decided to check out their set." (Anthony, p. 90).

Brothers sitting around talking about white bitches. Black Panther men exchanging notes on how to get their dicks sucked. Just because a sister is light skinned doesn't make her any less of a sister. It just means that she is more attractive to most white men and, unfortunately, to far too many black men. In many cases she a spoiled bitch who got the attention of her parents and was treated as "special" by many of her friends. I am simply documenting all this because any discussion of the black liberation movement rarely talks about the liberation of the mind when it came to white women; it talks about the black arts movement, black revolutionary nationalism, black cultural nationalism, bourgeois nationalism (as Alphonso Pinkney called one of the components) but they just can't seem to raise the issue of white women. Why? Because far too many were either sleeping with them or attracted to them.

And here's something for you to think about. When the peckerwood here and around the world wants to relax some kind of legally oppressive situation – whether you're talking about the apartheid system in South Africa or the Jim Crow system here in the U.S. – one of the first things they do is relax or dismiss the laws dealing with interracial marriage. This is an insult, but black people seem to view such an action as a sign of progress. White women have always been attracted to black men and would risk desk and flogging to get black dick. The white man knew it because he felt the same attraction when it came to both black women and black men. By freeing her up to fuck, the white male was simply creating another buffer that could protect him and his system from any real or perceived black "onslaught" that might take place.

Anthony writes that, "I had nothing against white women, and I had gone to bed with a great many of them during my Panther days, and it had always been a pleasant experience ... So I was game and looked forward to the date Hobbs had arranged for me with this French model." (p. 91). Do you still wonder why I titled this book, the demise of the black liberation movement? Although the topic at hand is the Black Panther Party, make no bones about it, this shit was taking place in other organizations with the possible exception of Karenga and his cultural nationalist US organization.

In far too many instances, Black people wanted to play Marxist and talk about "class struggle" so that they could convince white bitches that they were oppressed and, in doing so, get into the sack with them. This is the only logical explanation when you're tripping over beautiful young black women in order to lay next to a bitch with a flat ass, not tits, no lips and who at the time associated being "liberated" with not washing her pussy.

According to Earl Anthony, ""I told her I wanted to go to bed with her. We did, and as I did then, and always, because somehow I felt white women were more freakish than black women, I gave her oral sex first. Next we sixty-nined each other. Then I screwed her the natural way." (p. 92). What? He thinks it's "freaky" to suck pussy? Sistahs don't! The problem is they can't get too many of us to do it unless they've known us for a while and even then many of them have to ask (read: beg) for it! Anthony must have been raised around white people because he acts like one. It is almost as if he's boasting about his exploits with these women. What is there to brag about? Many, if not most, black men in this country have fucked at least one white women in their lives. It may have been clandestine (it most likely was), but it happens. The white man eventually finds out.

You just meet a bitch and you give her head and then engage in the "69" where you are mutually sucking each other off? What's wrong with this muthafucka? He didn't know this bitch. And the fact that she allowed it so quickly shows she's done it before which should raise some red flags! Her name was Michelle, so here is what happened, according to the race traitor Earl Anthony:

> "Michelle was loose, friendly, and we were soon sitting on the same sofa and French kissing. She then refused me sex, and I slapped her two or three times. I was overwhelmed by her and didn't wait to get back to the bedroom ... After I got an orgasm, I got on my knees and sucked Michelle's vagina." (Anthony, p. 128).

What's wrong with this muthafucka? He's working for the federal government as a snitch and he's committing sexual assaults! He's confessing to things (or lying about them) that most black men would be too ashamed to put in writing! What is his purpose for sharing this shit and confessing to the public what kind of muthafucka he is? How can he tell people that the U.S. government was paying him to fuck white women, snitch on black people and publish books confessing both? This is taxpayers' money we're talking about!

Michelle became "Shelley" and she was just as fucked up as he was. In fact, check out the following claims by Anthony and how he describes his on-going relationship with the white woman, "Shelley:"

> "Shelley knew I liked variety in women, so she introduced me that night to a beautiful white woman named June, who was in her mid-twenties and who Shelley said was a "black celebrity fucker." We drank together. June and I left together that night and went around to my hotel, the Statler Hilton. I had some pot and cocaine. Then June and I got naked -- we were very high by this time. We started having sex by doing the sixty-nine ... (Anthony, p. 130).

So this muthafucka is living at the Hilton on the government dole? He's living the life of Riley, has an apartment and a hotel room, walking around with money provided to him by people who hate black folks, having sex with white girls when he feels like it – and then writes about and publishes it? Did the publisher's check his sources? Did they bother to interview anyone from the FBI and ask about this asshole's credentials? So far all he's described is getting high and getting pussy. This second book,

Pissing in the Wind, which I am now quoting from, talks about the things he really didn't have the guts to talk about in his first book, which was called *Picking Up the Gun.* And even with that title, Dial Press published it. Why?

White people knew what they were doing. They were infatuated with the Black Panther Party and the black liberation movement. How else to explain the publishing of titles like *Die Nigger, Die; Revolutionary Suicide; To Die for the People; Negroes With Guns; Seize the Time* and so on? To sell books and to instigate the turmoil and tumult of the time period. The same can be said for the major newspapers: "if it bleeds, it leads" is a long time slogan that newspapers have passed on to their editors.

Anthony's second book reads like soft porn. And yet this is a man who served no time for anything. What about all the people that were jailed or even killed as a result of information that he provided to a racist government headed by a cross-dresser named J. Edgar Hoover?

> "I had three white women, who I was having sex with for free. They were nude dancers. We would have freak sex -- although I never did group sex. Then I met her, the white woman who I was almost to marry before I had my nervous breakdown later that year, 1974. She was the madame at a North Beach massage parlor. A young woman of Danish descent, who was five-feet ten inches tall and the most beautiful body I had ever seen. Her name was Christina, an she was a stunner ... (Anthony, p. 156).

So then, he admits that he paid for pussy. Not only is he a snitch, but he's also a trick. He is truly what we would call "whitey's nigger." He thinks like one, he talks like one and he acts like one. How did he get through the Panther leadership and end up telling them what to do and leading Huey's Defense Fund? It had to be the sheer ineptitude of the people who were calling themselves Panther leaders.

Look how he describes this white woman. He sounds like Eldridge Cleaver's descriptions in the book *Soul On Ice*. At any rate he loves whiteness and the idea of it. I view this as a form of misogyny because he hates black women but will still try to fuck them; I think he might even hate white women, and yet he longs for them. A "misogynist" is defined as, "a person who hates, dislikes, mistrusts, or mistreats women." So you can mistreat women by "loving" them for the wrong reasons, fucking them with ulterior motives (related to beastiality and what I call "thingification") or just view them in these idyllic terms just because of the color (or colorlessness) of their skin.

Realizing this, let us continue with the antics of Earl Anthony, the government informant:

> We started a whirlwind love affair. I went to the massage parlor every night for six months .... After Christina would get off at 2 a.m. we would go to breakfast and then to her apartment, where we would snort cocaine far into the morning, and then we would have freak sex. I always felt that I had to suck off a white woman." (Anthony, pp. 156-157)

What purpose is there in sharing this information? What does he hope to gain? Any white woman with self-respect would probably resent him going public with such information. And it's not even so much that he felt he "had" to suck off a white woman; it was the fact that this white bitch enjoyed it, allowed it and after getting high on coke, sat back and accepted it. No mention is made of what we all know, however: that she was sucking his dick as well. And that leads to another question: why does he only mention getting head when it involves mutual "69" action. What's wrong: do him have a witty-bitty weenie?

But don't get it twisted: Earl Anthony was an equal opportunity sexist and abuser. Not only was he fascinated with white women, he also abused and disrespected black women. The record speaks for itself:

> "It was the month before May, and I was back in New York waiting for my book to come out, when the Mafia ran the "looper" at me. I had a friend who was a barmaid at Pee Wee's jazz nightclub ... her name was Shelley .... A "looper" is what it is called when the Mafia checks you out to see if they want to pick you up to work for them ... (Anthony, p. 70).

So this muthafucka not only worked for the racist FBI, but also appears to be connected or at least considered by, organized crime. And he's writing about it. And nobody presses any charges or the very least the Panthers could have done was call a press conference and do to the FBI was they FBI was doing to them: let the public know about the underhanded infiltration tactics that were being practiced and promoted by the Bureau. Why didn't the women whose first names he is so freely throwing around file a defamation suit or perhaps get together and do some class action filing? At very minimum they could have exposed the FBI and what was being done. But the women – much like the Panther leadership -- didn't do shit.

At any rate, this sexually twisted asshole continues his story:

> After the pictures of [Boomer, a bald headed black woman] ... were shown around, she sat on the top of the bar and pulled up her dress. She was wearing no panties, and had a bare vulva. She announced: "I've got the prettiest pussy in New York! Who wants to eat it?" I shouted, "I do." Everybody laughed ... Boomer and I went to the bedroom. She asked me to tie her to the bed with the sheets and fuck her. I did. She would cry out: "Harder! Harder! I came three times, then Boomer and James left... (Anthony, p. 73).

So I was right: he is dickless. That's why he relies so heavily on sucking pussy. But this is a black woman and she don't just want the lips – she wants the hips! Yellling "harder, harder" means that the pussy has opened up because she's gotten a nut. And it's up to you to get some friction action going on the pussy lips, coupled with some deep thrusts. And it seems to me that Anthony couldn't handle it – another reason why he probably prefers white bitches. The stereotype of the "big black dick" feeds into their mindset so even if you don't have one, the psychological reaction so skin color and the nappy head will serve to make her get a nut one way or the other.

Enter another white woman -- this one named Robin:

> When we got there, Robin had some pot so I smoked some with her. I asked her to have sex with me, but she refused. I used a tactic that had become a fetish with women I particularly loved ... I slapped her had two or three times. She relented then, and I made her give me oral sex first and then I went inside of her. (Anthony, p. 74).

This was a rape, and that bitch fed into it. This man is admitting that he assaulted a woman – a white woman at that – and nobody who read this shit gave a fuck enough to have charges filed. Why not? It would be a case of this fuckin' traitor getting what he deserved. But if he used the tactic before and the bitches gave up the pussy, then they're just as goony as he is.

This guy is not only a dope fiend, but he's got some sexual addiction issues as well. And he's getting paid to act out all of his problems in the name of being a snitch. Pay attention to the following:

> "While working as a consultant for the Board, I began a love affair with a black school teacher named Janet. It wasn't long before Robin began to sense I was having an affair. It made her angry, starting many of our arguments. The love affair with Janet continued. We would check into midtown hotels many days after she had finished teaching at her school." (Anthony, p. 96).

Was he "going with" or engaged to Robin? No. So then, how could he be having "an affair" behind her back? They were both single and therefore available. Here's what I think: I think it's because Robin was white there was an unspoken belief that he had better be "committed" to her and her whiteness. And the fact that he finally had some feelings from someone of his own race felt like a "double betrayal" to her. First of all, because she had been sucking his dick all this time and secondly, because, after all, she was a white woman! How dare this nigger mess around with one of his own when he has *me* to fuck and suck on!

And here's a question: why is he checking into midtown hotels with the sister when he has a place of his own and a hotel room? Was he afraid the white woman would find them? Was he hiding from Robin? Here's an answer:

> "The arguments with Robin continued and some nights I would leave the apartment angry and go to Times Square, and into the topless bars to catch a show with the naked girls; and often I would pick up a black prostitute. I could always go for a little sleaze." (Anthony, p. 96).

Who is this muthafucka to refer to any situation that he is involved in as "sleaze" as if its somehow out of the norm? He IS a fuckin' sleaze; Earl Anthony is the personification of all that is sleazy, politically, socially and sexually. He's the antithesis of what any sane black person would want his or her son to grow up to be. In simpler terms, he's a piece of shit. When arguments take place, you run from the woman you claim to love. Where is the first place you go? You head to a topless bar. What do you find in a topless bar? Sleazy patrons and scurvy bitches. And yet you feel comfortable in such an environment; you feel that this is the place to run to for relaxation. So tell me: doesn't that make this asshole just about as sleazy as they come?

And what difference does it make that the prostitute is black? His white woman was a prostitute, the women he was sucking and fucking were prostitutes and former prostitutes. The Black Panther Party was filled with both male and female prostitutes. What he wrote was a statement deliberately aimed at taking a shot at black women. Remember this is a man who described one white woman as, "A young woman of Danish descent, who was five-feet ten inches tall and the most beautiful body I had ever seen. Her name was Christina, an she was a stunner." He hates himself, he hates black people and as a result, he's the perfect foil for snitching and betraying folks that the American system orders him to betray. And he does it in exchange for money. So tell me: when all is said and done, who's the REAL prostitute?

Back to Robin:

> "To please her ... I decided to take her to San Francisco. We stayed at the fashionable Miyako Hotel. But the argument continued so I went out the first night and found a prostitute. Robin left me that night saying she was going to Denver to stay with her friend, Shyleen." (Anthony, p. 100).

How did they get the money to stay at the Miyako? Who paid? And why were these arguments continuing? Again, these disagreements seem to take place and then this coward runs out the door and buys some pussy. So the issue isn't about pussy is it? Why would you leave a nice hotel like the Miyako because of an argument unless you had an ulterior motive? This asshole has a sexual addiction and if Robin doesn't jump when he says jump (or suck when he says suck), then he's out the door looking for new pussy. Robin, like most women, got tired of his bullshit, and all I can say is that it took her long enough.

So now Robin is out and later on he describes other sexcapades and again, he's quick to point out the element of "race." This particular one takes place out of the country:

> "The driver waited and slept outside, while we went into the Kenyan woman's house, and we had straight sex (African women, at least at that time, didn't do different sexual positions, or oral sex). The next day, after my first sexual experience with an African woman, and my fourth day in the country, I returned to the hotel ... "(Anthony, p. 110).

He's right about African women for the most part. They can be programmed to give up some head, but that takes time. Only the sluttish ones give it up on the first date. In far too many cases many of them are forced into sex by brutish African men. I've had three African wives so I know what I'm talking about. At any rate, he falls for this African chick:

> "I had tired of womanizing for the moment, but in Stephanie -- that was her name -- I was able to get my fill of lovemaking. She had the same excellent qualities, sensually, that I found in all black women, American, Caribbean and African." (Anthony, p. 113)

He calls what he does "womanizing"? He screws women who are whores by lying to them and then when they show that they have a brain or have grown tired of his bullshit, he cuts and runs. That's not a womanizer: that's a coward! He sounds shacks that an African sistah would have "excellent qualities," but he qualifies that statement by limiting that quality to "sensually" speaking. In other words, she's a good fuck, and that's how this muthafucka sees all women. And that's why he's a piece of shit and people who read his book should be able to recognize that. This is the same way that the white man depicts his macho hero types: you know, the lone wolf who gets lots of pussy while gunning people down and saving entire groups. Lies – all lies.

Now we come to the real nature of this cowardly bastard as is indicated in the following excerpt:

> "I was getting high on cognac, and so was she, and she finally told me, cautiously: "I am in love with somebody else. His name is Melvin Briscoe and he lives in Denver." I went into a blind rage and began beating her in the body with karate chops. This went on for what seemed like an hour, until she passed out. Later, she told me that I had fractured her ribs. When she regained consciousness, we had sex; then I took her to the airport for her flight back to Denver. I knew I had lost her." (Anthony, p. 116).

Was there any doubt? Those African bitches don't play that "beat me I'm still conscious" type shit that these American bitches, black and white, tend to practice. But let's look at the previous paragraph and get a more profound understanding of male actions and psychology in general, and Earl Anthony in particular.

First of all, he was "getting high" on cognac but the African sistah was just getting a buzz. She was probably from a country that was a French colony so it only stands to reason that she would be drinking some top shelf shit. Secondly, she must have been a slut: if she was in love with somebody else, why was she fucking around with a loser like Anthony? Why was she drinking cognac with this man when she has a man in Denver. And third, why is she telling Anthony where her man lives? What's wrong with this bitch.

Then we get to point four: why would he go into a blind rage? He wasn't in love with this sistah – she was just a piece of pussy as far as he was concerned. So what was his fuckin' problem? He beat her in the body the way a pimp would do, because they don't like to scar up a woman's face, lest she call the cops. Then the bitch shows how sick she is by fucking him even though she has broken ribs! Then he takes her to the airport so she can fly to Denver and go back to her boyfriend having just fucked another guy, something women have been getting away with for centuries.

From there it was a continuation of the same dog-ass shit he had always done:

> I began to womanize again as soon as I got to San Francisco in August, 1971, and moved into Alonzo X's apartment. For a while I dated an old flame, television commentator Carolyn Cravens ... Then there was Janice Cobb, who was to become a medical doctor; Carrie Mae, who worked as a secretary for a black dentist friend of mine who was also a publisher; Hattie, president of the Black Student Union at California State University, Hayward ... and Penny, who worked at San Francisco State University (p. 124).

Doesn't anybody read any more? Why don't these bitches sue this man? What he's saying about them is libelous and slanderous. He's fucking these women, some of them who are victims of violence, which makes it sexual assault. Then he writes a book and the white publishers, hoping to sell books, don't even edit the names out of the fuckin' text? Not only does he name the women but he names their locations! So he was a snitch when it came to the Panthers and he's a damn sellout and an informant when it comes to the private lives of black and white women. He admits he buys pussy, which is a misdemeanor, and earlier he admits that he broke a woman's ribs. What more is needed?

And in this case, what is the common denominator? Anthony tells us that, "All these chicks were black, and this lasted from August to November, 1971, with me interchanging between the women, until I met Cynthia Watson, a fine, dark-complexioned student who was to become my steady lady." (Brown, p. 124). Did he tell her what a piece of shit he was? Did she already know? Couldn't she tell by the way he carried himself that he was not worth a plugged nickel? On the same page of the book he writes that, "I love women, but it was more than just that; it was also because I had lost my first wife, Robin, that I was on an ego trip with women." (p. 124). What a liar.

He doesn't love women: he loves the *idea* of women and he loves abusing them. When he leaves one he likes the feeling of knowing that he's duped yet another one. I know that feeling quite well. Many of us are raised around men who have a lot of women and the respect that they get for having them. It seems to be a goal, a method of operation of the average kid to have "a bunch of bitches." I know I did. But one thing I did not do was lie to them about them being "the only one." Most of them knew that they were not. The greatest "dis-respector" of women is not the womanizer, the pimp or the playa; it's other women.

Next comes a convenient "excuse" (rather than an explanation):

> "Years later when I was going through psychiatric therapy, the conclusion was reached that not only was I high off alcohol every time I beat a woman, but I had picked up the habit from my environment." (Anthony, p. 124).

He's a lying sack of shit. "Every time" he beat a woman he was drunk? Or did he have to get drunk in order to get an erection? Then, in vintage white boy psychiatrist fashion, what do they blame? They blame "the environment." In other words, the ghetto, other niggas, fucked up daddy issues, mommy not home, and so on. When it's white boys it's a "disease;" when it's niggas it's a "tangle of pathology" or a "culture of deprivation." No muthafucka: you were genetically fucked up because of being a freak of nature. Nobody could sell out their own race and then treat women the way Earl Anthony did unless he had something seriously wrong with his brain stem.

> "John Horn, Jack Willis, and myself were friends in the early 1960s in San Francisco. John Horn was a pimp, with a prostitute named Jamaica. Several times with Jack, I would be over at John Horn's and he would beat Jamaica to make her put on a lesbian show for us with another chick who we would have picked up. Then John would let us screw Jamaica, and of course, the other chicks; it was called "chippying." (Anthony, pp. 124-125).

He's trying to scapegoat some street bruthas and pawn their lifestyles and perversions off on influencing him turning into the piece of shit that he would become. First of all, how did they become "friends"? Probably over the dope game or some other crime. So that means Anthony made a conscious choice. When he found out that John was a pimp and kept hanging with him, that means that he made a conscious choice to do so. When he found out that Jamaica was selling her body, which is against the law, not only did he not do anything but he would screw her himself. He would watch women screwing each other and get off on it after watching John assault her. *All of this is criminal behavior that I am sure the FBI knew or learned about when they put Anthony on the payroll.* They knew that if the money they paid him to sell out his own race was not enough, they could always arrange to throw some pussy at him.

He was a trick, a pervert and that meant that he was a perfect male candidate for the Black Panther Party. Check it out:

> "I had gone to bed with so many prostitutes in the Fillmore area of San Francisco that I became known by name. Then a bad thing happened. I had sex with a black prostitute, then pulled a gun on her, and told her I wasn't paying. It was about 1967, when I was with the Black Panthers, and we controlled the streets of San Francisco. And the next time I had sex with a black whore in the Fillmore district, I did the same thing. Neither time did I rob them because I had money." (Anthony, p. 125).

This muthafucka wrote about this and not a single person who read the book bothered to follow up on the on-going misdemeanors and felonies he committed? He was robbing sistahs who were out there trying to earn a living. He was in possession of an unlicensed firearm. He was a member of the Black Panther Party and didn't seem to give a shit about anyone in the organization. If there was ever a black person who should be taken out and shot in the fuckin' head at dawn, it's Earl Anthony. And now I've put MY feelings in writing. Deal with it.

Continuing:

> "When I came back to San Francisco in August, 1971, there was a whole flock of new black whores who didn't know me. I began to run them, although I was, at the same time, having sex with my regular girl friends, including freakish Carrie Mae, who loved oral sex. I've always said until recently that I loved women with "a little dog in her." That

> refers to a raw woman; and the prostitutes with their mini-skirts, boots, and bold stances on the corners, got up my sexual nature. (Anthony, p. 125).

"New flock of black whores"? Not only is this insultingly animalistic terminology, but it's also discriminatory. How does he know their whores? Prostitutes get paid for fuckin' so the whore is the male who is buying the pussy, not her. A whore is a woman that gives it up for free. Can you look at a woman and tell if she's a whore or not? Of course not – that is, unless you are of the mindset that all women are whores. And I believe this is at the root of Earl Anthony's thinking.

He enjoys licking pussy – just like the white man does. And as I state earlier, that is because he is lacking in the dick department. How else to explain licking on something that smells that way, giving the woman pleasure (supposedly) while you get up with your breath and upper lip smelling like halibut? He was a trick – the women, at least the black ones, were identifying him as "the brutha that eats pussy." That is not a compliment for the most part – but of course, they're glad to have someone "go down to the Y" and save them the time of washing off sperm running down their leg after a healthy fuckin.'

> "Whenever I didn't have a date to go to dinner, drink, smoke marijuana, snort cocaine, and have sex, I would go buy a prostitute. In fact, there was a high yellow complexioned black prostitute in her twenties named Judy, who used to wear her mini-skirts up her naked behind, who I started to pimp. I liked her because she liked me, and when I started to buying her, she wouldn't play by the prostitute game; that is whenever you had an orgasm you would have to get up. I would keep fucking Judy after I came, until I got a second orgasm. Then we would lay in bed and talk ... (Anthony, pp. 125- 126).

To add to his long list of crimes that he committed while working for the FBI mind you, he can now add pimping. He's bragging about licking pussy the way most black men brag (and probably lie) about using their dicks. This shows that he's willing to give women he hardly knows an orgasm, but at the same time he's willing to sell an entire race of people out to the FBI, which was then as now notoriously known for hunting down, locking up, and shooting down black men who talked about freedom and liberation.

He's paying for pussy using taxpayers money! Didn't any of these bitches ever bother to ask this ass wipe where he worked? Or who he was employed by? Didn't they give a shit? Of course, we are talking about the 1970s. Today's women sure would! They'd be running background and credit checks on this muthafucka. And not only that, but a nigga who licks pussy would raise red flags in the minds of most black women because they know bruthas aren't prone to that sort of thing. But it was a different time, and sellouts like Anthony were able to play upon the collective naivete and new-found black consciousness and social conscience of a lot of people – both black and white.

The name-dropping and on-going disrespect by Earl Anthony continues:

> "I contacted black dance professor Dolores Cayou, who had brought me to San Francisco State University to be her professional colleague ... I was excited by our fruitful work night, and although she didn't partake, I was high from drinking wine and smoking dope. I asked her to go to bed with me, because I was crazy about her. She said that she had a boyfriend. I was infuriated and beat her and forced her to have sex with me ... (Anthony, p. 133).

If the bitch "had a boyfriend," then why was she cavorting and drinking wine with Anthony? These bitches seem to think that they have everything so much under control that they can invite a man up to their apartment, drink wine, walk around with a dress up the crack of their ass, and then when things get too hot, claim to have a boyfriend. Any man knows that if there was anything serious going on with that "boyfriend," then why do I have my ass up here in your apartment? But to do what Anthony did – bogart the pussy and beat the shit out of the woman until you get it – that is a felonious assault. That is outright rape. And again, he's writing and bragging about it.

At no point does Anthony discuss divorcing any of the "wives" he's had. Elsewhere in the book Elaine writes about a Panther divorce where were told that if two people were in the Party and were married, they didn't have to go the official route in getting a divorce. According to Elaine, "all they needed to do was repeat six times, "I divorce you, I divorce you, I divorce you," making 360-degree turns as they did so, and they would be divorced. Maybe that was what he was talking about. At any rate, Anthony's degradation campaign continues:

> "It was during this time that I was to meet a young woman who was to become my second wife. She was a nineteen year old black student who had an infant son ... She was a dancer and my best student ... One day I invited her to a San Francisco nightclub, to see a black group, young women who called themselves French Toast. They wanted me to manage them … (Anthony, p. 133).

Either Anthony is embellishing his life or he's lying so much that he's getting confused. Doesn't the bitch have a name? Why not mention it as you describe her as being on the cusp of being your second wife? And furthermore, why would these women want him to be their manager – that is, unless by "manager" they mean "pimp"? Furthermore, this particular woman has a child, but does that stop Anthony from his fucked up ways? Of course not. Check out what he does to this woman who he supposedly has these deep feelings for:

> After the performance I invited her to my apartment. We smoked marijuana, and talked. Early in the morning I made a move to her. She refused and headed to the door. I caught her and slapped her hard several times. I had sex with her that night and instantly she became my girlfriend." (Anthony, p. 133).

What kinds of bitches are these? Do they just play hard to get and therefore think that a right to the jaw is some form of love? Or is this muthafucka lying and making it look like sistahs are taking this kind of abuse? Educated sisters – not white bitches, which history shows us will take an ass whipping for a black dick any day.

At any rate, what kind of man would want a woman like this for his girlfriend? If logic stands, then the guy who comes along who hits her the hardest will be able to take her away from Anthony! No wonder he equates violence with power and love and that would explain why he'd become the ideal Panther officer. But throughout his books, both of them, he doesn't mention throwing down with any men, black or white. He doesn't challenge any of the bruthas. This is another one of his white characteristics: avoiding the male of the species and taking your anger out on the woman. Earl Anthony is a cowardly piece of shit. It has little to do with "environment;" this shit is *genetic*.

This would explain why he has no mention of his mother or father in either book. He doesn't want anyone coming along and doing research on his family tree. He doesn't mention and brothers, sisters or cousins. This is the sign of someone who has something to hide, and having read what I've read, and realizing that he must be some kind of masochist to write about the crimes he's committed and to provide the names of the people that he has abused, he has every reason to live his life in shame.

Moving on:

> "I had received a letter from Robin that she was having a baby by another man and wanted a divorce. She did get a divorce on the grounds of mental and physical cruelty. She also got a police restraining order so that I could not go near her, as it was legally adjudged that I had physically abused her in the past." (Anthony, p. 134).

Finally, we get to a divorce. But she couldn't have filed it by herself. He would have had to sign some papers and would have had to be present. How can he omit such information – unless he's telling yet another bold-faced lie? Robin finally came to her senses, but the restraining order doesn't trump the fact that he has paperwork to fill out. And as I've been saying in this book, just like it could be "legally adjudged" that this asshole had physically abused Robin, the same could easily be done by those other women. They might collectively even have a class action since Anthony wrote about what he did, how he did it and since he's already hated by just about every black person in the Bay Area. But alas, t'was not to be.

According to Anthony,

> "There was only one incident to mar our beautiful relationship. For some obscure reason she had to pass up seeing me on my birthday; and when I saw her the next night I got angry and slapped her, blackening both of her eyes. I was mostly seeing Gayle on weekends but during the week I was still having sexual encounters with the San Francisco whores, mostly Judy who did not charge me any money ... Judy and I finally had a big argument about Gayle, and I had to beat her, not just slap her, because she fought back. I was never to see her again." (Anthony, p. 140).

When a man writes a book where he has established a pattern of beating, maiming and assaulting women on this level, shouldn't the publisher be liable for this shit? Wasn't there a law about allowing someone who has broken the law to profit from having broken those laws? Assaulting women is a fuckin' crime, I don't care if you live in San Francisco or New York. He's giving women black eyes, breaking their ribs and rendering major pain on them and he still finds people who read it, publish it and then do nothing about it. What then, does this say about the American public? And what does it say about Black Panther members and supporters, past and present, would allow a sick fuck like Earl Anthony to go around besmirching the name of the Party by associating himself with them as he engages in these sick and sadistic escapades?

So now Gayle gets pregnant. Why would a woman get pregnant by a nigga like this? Was she desperate? Why would he, knowing his lack of character, want to bring a life into the world knowing full well that he would most likely fuck that life up as he had done so many others? He claims that,

> "I was filled with bliss; my first child about to come. I never physically abused Gayle during he pregnancy, and never touched another woman sexually, although I did go to Washington, D.C. while Gayle and I were together to see Robin ..." (Anthony, p. 149).

Where is he getting all this money to travel back and forth between bitches, to secure apartments and buy all this pussy? I'll tell you where: from your hard-earned money! Does he mention having a job anywhere? Is he punching a clock? Does he carry a brief case or go to the cleaners to pick up his suits? No. He just walks around and remember, in those days there was no "automatic deposit." So the Federal government was sending checks to this asshole at some unknown address and he was cashing them. Either that, or this man is the biggest liar in the history of the known universe. You do the math and start asking some logical questions for a change.

Earl Anthony was the perfect pick to be a sellout and snitch. He had no values and was lacking in morals. Where he got his habits and views, I don't know but I know this: he learned a lot of what he did from white folks and the rest is just based on self-hate. For instance, take note of the following:

> "But as soon as the baby was born I began my womanizing again. It began with a lovely, dark-complexioned black student, who a few years after was to become a highly paid model ... It was at my office where this young black woman struck a pose at the door. I knew who it was immediately because she was considered the most beautiful woman on campus ... (Anthony, p. 150).

What campus was this muthafucka on? What does he mean "his office"? What degrees or credentials did this loser have to get a job on campus where he would have his own office? And who were the people who considered this black woman the most beautiful on campus? What does Anthony do? He engages in what today would be referred to as "sexual harassment," but even back then it was not ethical – and was grounds for termination – to be dating students.

Check it out:

> I asked her to come help me celebrate and asked her out to dinner and drinks. We went to a seafood place. All I could talk about was my first child. From dinner we went to my apartment, which was furnished lavishly. There, we drank wine, smoked marijuana, and snorted cocaine. I asked this beautiful young student to go to bed, and she immediately agreed." (Anthony, p. 150).

What "lavish" apartment? How was it furnished? Whose selected the furniture? But a bigger question: how is this bitch-built muthafucka surviving? He's buying pussy, buying dinners, he's getting jobs on college campuses, buying wine and plenty of weed. And he's confessing to all this. And remember: this is not a fiction or a novel – this is autobiographical. This muthafucka oughta be put UNDER the jail!

Now he's gone to bed with a student, a direct ethical violation (but these college professors are doing it all the time). According to this asshole, his escapades would continue:

> "After we got back to Washington, I was to continue my womanizing. Not only was I having sex with Gayle, and the beautiful student who would become a famous model, but I started "hanging" on the whore stroll in D.C. Most of the whores, if they didn't know me, would ask, "Are you a pimp or the police?" They would ask me this because of my fancy clothes. After I told them I was neither, they would say, "Show me your dick!" Evidently the police couldn't do that. I would show them my penis. Then I would pick up one of the whores." (Anthony, pp. 151-152).

This is an old prostitute trick for you square out there. If you show a prostitute your dick, then you can't bust her just in case you happen to be an undercover cop. It's like dope dealers; if you come in to cop, they make you smoke a joint or take a hit or shoot some dope in front of them and in that way your testimony, if you're a cop or a snitch, becomes totally inadmissible.

At any rate, this guy is nothing more than a trick for the government, an embarrassment to any black man worth his salt. White boys, I can understand: they are the ones who have made prostitution the world's oldest profession. Most of them have no game or no rap and the ones who do learned it from us. So they have to pay for pussy and in that way, when they prematurely ejaculate or expose a shrunken dick, the bitch can't complain or laugh because she's being paid to lie and feed this asshole's urges, which includes his ego. See? You learn something every day, don't you? Let's move on with the stories of the most morally bankrupt muthafucka I have ever heard or read about:

> "I did continue to have affairs with other women, even with my former wife, Robin, who was now in Denver. The tension was high between Gayle and me, and a couple of times I resorted to slapping her. I was miserable, because I loved Gayle and my new family. But I would drink, smoke dope, and snort cocaine, and I would get high and become violent toward Gayle who would try unsuccessfully to fight me back. " (Anthony, pp. 152-153).

I suppose I should be fair and share the following with you: even though, as have shown, Earl Anthony is a piece of shit, the women he chose to deal with – the ones who made the decision to submit to his advances – are also fucked up. These bitches let that nigga assault them and didn't call the cops. They let him maim them and didn't report the incident to the hospital officials (I'm assuming that the African sistah whose reibs he fractured had to go to the hospital or some medical facility). And they fell for his bullshit lines and tactics. They indirectly and directly sold him pussy, which let him know their lack of character from jump street. So like takes to like. But as a "brutha" and as a Panther (fake, of course), he had an obligation to at least value the privacy of these women. Instead, what does he do? He writes a book and spills his guts, gives out their names and maligns their character. He is truly the lowest of the low.

Anthony makes it sound as if he is some kind of "God's gift to women" and that women have no rights that he is bound to respect. For instance, check out the following:

> "Gayle balked every time I started biting at the rein to get out of the apartment on my own. I wanted to do some womanizing -- if only with whores ... Finally one of the arguments developed into a fight, and I slapped Gayle around pretty badly. With that, she left me and took the

> children to Buffalo, New York, to stay with some of her
> relatives." (Anthony, p. 155).

One has to see that Gayle was a piece of shit herself. She allowed this shit to go on with children to think about. And she had these children by one of the lowest human beings who ever existed. He could have contracted a venereal disease and brought it home to her. She must not have been all that attentive because if he was aching to leave, it wasn't just because of her. He didn't want to have anything to do with the kids that he earlier claimed he loved so much. Again, he got his way through the use of violence and Gayle did the only thing she could: she left and went away to New York. Now he could be alone and get all the pussy he wanted, since that seems to be all that he was living for.

But he had money, no morals and evidently high energy. So after Gayle left check out what took place:

> "I flew to Jamaica for the Christmas holidays and on the
> flight to the island, I ran into a young black woman named
> Libra, who was in the first class section with me. I gave
> her a couple of autographed copies of my book and upon
> landing in Jamaica, we caught a cab together ... I went to
> meet her boss, black jazz musician Miles Davis, who was
> staying in a villa outside of Ocho Rios. It was to be an
> eventful night of conversation, as Miles and I swapped
> words. I had to sneak in and make love to Libra while
> Miles slept with another woman. Miles saw how attentive
> Libra was to me the next day, and asked me to leave."
> (Anthony, p. 155).

Now he brings Miles into it. Now Miles was no angel, but one thing I can say about him: he had a high level of black consciousness. When I reviewed his book, *Miles,* back in 1990 as the editor of the *Milwaukee Courier* newspaper, I was impressed with it. He called it like he saw it, including letting people know that while Cicely Tyson plays all those "black roles" and has people thinking she gives a shit about black people, she is actually a sellout and she was the one who provided him with drugs when he needed them. He also shared a little story about the late Milton Berle which I find somewhat relevant here.

As Miles recalls,

> I remember one time when Milton Berle, the comedian,
> came down to me when I was playing at the Three Deuces.
> I was in Bird's band at the time. I think this was in 1948.

> Anyway, Berle was sitting at a table listening to us and somebody asked him what he thought of the band and the music. He laughed and turned to this group of white people he was with and said that we were "headhunters," meaning we were fucking savages. He thought it was funny, and I remember all those white people laughing at us. (Davis, 1989: 406)

This is why I write. Like Miles, I want black people to know what is going on behind the doors of the places that they might not be able to get into. Places I can get into because I have degrees, and have held a few high status positions. And I want them to know that no matter how much that job paid or how well I was doing, I stood up for what we, as a people, stand for. I am the polar opposite of that piece of shit Earl Anthony, which is just the kind of nigga that white people use, exploit and enjoy promoting.

Miles' recollection of the Berle incident continues:

> Well, I never forgot that. Then I saw him on an airplane about twenty-five years after that and we were both riding in first class. I went up and introduced myself to him. I said, "Milton, my name is Miles Davis and I'm a musician." He started smiling and said, "Oh, yeah, I know who you are. I really love your music." He seemed happy that I had come up to him." (Davis.,p. 407)

Then, Miles lowered the boom:

> Then I said, "Milton, you did something to me and some people in the band I was playing with some years ago that I've always remembered, and I always told myself that if I ever got close enough to breathe on you that I was gonna tell you the way I felt when you said what you said that night." He was looking at me kin of funny now because he didn't know what he had said. And I could feel some of the anger of that night coming back so it must have been showing in my face. I told him what he said and I told him how they had all laughed at us. Now his face was turning red because he was embarrassed, and he had probably forgotten all about it. So then I told him, "I don't like what you called us that night, Milton, and none of the band liked it either after I told them what you said. Some of them also heard what you said." He looked all pitiful and everything and then he said, "I'm very, very sorry." And I said, "I know you are. But you're only sorry now, sorry after I told

> you, because you weren't sorry then." And then I turned
> around and went back to my seat and sat down and didn't
> say another word to him (David, 1989, p. 407).

Just like you wouldn't know about this piece of shit Earl Anthony and the sexism that permeated the Black Panther Party were it not for me and my vast scholarship, so it is with dispelling the myth of "Uncle Miltie," as he was known. He might have been some kind of clown prince of comedy to white boys and Jews, but you see what he thinks about us. And I mention this for an important reason as it relates to Earl Anthony and his trip to Jamaica.

Miles took to Anthony because it is clear that the snitch has the gift of gab. Miles trusted that muthafucka because there's no telling how many lies he (Anthony) told in order to curry favor with the late jazz great. Now according to Anthony, "Miles saw how attentive Libra was to me the next day, and asked me to leave." More than likely this is bullshit. Libra was obviously easy pussy and Miles could fuck any woman he wanted. He had no reason to be jealous of a piece of shit like Anthony, nothing more than a fuckin' *turista*. What happened, in my estimation, is that Miles saw through this nigga as being a fake, a front and a charlatan and sickened of him, figuring that once he got ahold of some island pussy he would never leave.

So Miles, being the straightforward person that he was (hence the previous quote regarding Milton Berle) more likely than not told the nigga to "get ta steppin'." And Anthony, being the cowardly asshole he is who only beats up on women, saw that Miles wasn't bullshitting and took off – leaving the pussy totally behind. That's what I think.

Back to Earl Anthony, who claims, "I went to see Christina to tell her I would be with Gayle and the kids for a few weeks. We got into an argument, and I slapped her. I would never see her again." (p. 158). Slapping these women around shows how fortunate Anthony is – he was slapping around on the right bitches. The women I know, at least some of them, he would have raised his hand and drawn back a gnub. Even back then in the 1970s and '80s there were women who didn't take that shit.

Maybe it's young bitches he was choosing who didn't know anything about life. But once a man hits you and if you do nothing, he'll do it again. And it is for that reason I don't buy into that shit about you should "never hit a woman." Fuck that. You should never hit a woman FIRST. But if a bitch hits you, hit her ass back. If you don't she won't respect you and she'll see your non-response as a green light to do it again. Furthermore, they claim to be so "equal," so stop treating them like they're children or some kind of "soft inferiors." If they got guts enough to hit you while knowing full well that they are attracted to you for your strength, then they got the guts to pay the piper when they make that decision. I'm just sayin'.

Continuing on:

> "Meanwhile, in August, some business came up in regard to Alexander the Great's and I had to fly to New York. I took Gayle and the children with me. On the plane I started talking to Gayle about my other women. We began to argue. I slapped Gayle, and to my surprise, she slapped me back. We continued to argue and fight all the way cross the country. When we landed at JFK, I slapped Gayle so many times that I knocked her to the ground, then I kicked her in the side." (Anthony, p. 158).

Where was the security? How is this black muthafucka slapping on this woman and how is she being allowed to fight him back? Why didn't she summon help? Why do bitches think they can over power a man that is already kicking their ass? Today, in 2015, some of the people who teach women self-defense are telling them that if they are attacked, just lay back and take it. If the best you can do is a slap that is only going to antagonize the man who is assaulting you, then maybe that's the best advice.

In this case you see what Anthony is claiming: these niggas are embarrassing the hell out of themselves and black people in general. Fighting in an air port with the kids watching? Why would he slap her in the first place. Did she express an opinion that ran counter to his? This guy needs to be locked up – no, not necessarily in the pen where he would get dicked in the ass which he would probably like – but in an asylum so he could be analyzed and perhaps drugged. He knocks this woman down, puts the boot to her, and not a single muthafucka comes to her aid.

Later that same day, Anthony claims the following took place:

> "That evening, after being out all day on business with financiers for my projects, I found a package in my mail box. It was some sex stamina pills that I had ordered from the September, 1974 issue of *Penthouse* magazine, the last time I was in the New York apartment. The pills had come from Los Angeles. I wanted them because I had promised Christina in San Francisco that I would start sex orgying with her and her friends. I took several of the stamina pills because I was going woman hunting that night … (p. 158).

Sex stamina pills. All that bragging and boasting, all this talk about fucking and sucking and now I think we have the key: stamina pills. How else would he know the address. The issue of Penthouse went all the way back to 1974 when he was fucking around with Elaine Brown and some other Panther bitches. So that's how he got it down. That's one thing he forgot to mention. And another thing he forgot to mention while talking about all that "sex orgying" he was planning on doing, was the first mention of his mama and his daddy:

> It was LSD. I started tripping. I had had LSD before but never any as powerful as this ... The next morning I flew to Los Angeles. My mother and father, Geraldine and James Anthony, picked me up at the airport, taking me straight to the mental ward of UCLA." (Anthony, pp. 158-159).

The pills that came in the mail were LSD tablets? Nigga, please! He took it knowing what it was and he should have expected to trip out. I remember taking one tab of Orange Sunshine back in 1973 and even a decade later I'd occasionally see flashes of light in the corners of my eyes. That shit is unpredictable, which is why it is known as a hallucinogenic drug. But just as I recommended earlier, his actions proved he was a fuckin' and his mama and daddy evidently knew it. There is no doubt in my mind that it must have run in the family!

With the editing and writing skills of a retarded circus monkey, there are no real details about what happened when he got to the looney bin. But one thing is for sure: he continued teaching. Ain't that a bitch? And you wonder why American education is 13th in the world today in 2016? I'll tell you why: the muthafuckas doing the hiring are either on the downlow, lesbians or perverts and they hire people who they feel will "accommodate" them, if you know what I mean. That's the only way to explain it: no group of decision makers who do hiring at the post-secondary level could be this collectively fucked up in those decisions unless there was something political or sexual going on.

The hatred of women, interracial sex and on-going abuse of both black and white women capsulize this chapter. And remember: it's consistent which means it's a part of his nature:

> "As spring of 1976 came in, I was still teaching. My substance abuse did not affect my performance at the workplace. I was doing well there. It was during that time, though, that Gayle and I got into an argument over my problem, but I didn't slap her. I wrestled her to the floor

and began to karate chop her in the ribs. She left that night with the kids to stay with my brother Ronald and his wife Renee for a few days." (Anthony, pp. 165-166).

That is such bullshit when he claims that his substance abuse didn't affect his work. The only way that would be true was if his work was so fucked up that the drugs didn't make a difference. And judging from how fucked up he is in the head and in his life, it's a possibility that he was also a goon in the classroom as well.

And where does this muthafucka get the nerve to talk about giving these women "karate chops"? What does he know about the martial arts? Maybe he gave them a pork chop and got it confused! But if he was so adept in fighting, why didn't the cowardly sonofabitch jump on some of those bruthas that were insulting him? Why didn't he confront that guy in Denver who the African woman told him about (instead of kicking her all up in the ass)? He's a typical coward who, when no one is around, wants to sound like he's the hog with the big nuts. But in reality, he's a limp piece of shit, licking a whole lot of pussy and taking dick stamina pills in order to get off. This, in my view, is the legacy of the sellout bastard who wrote books with the grandiose titles, *Picking Up the Gun* in 1970 and *Spitting in the Wind* twenty years later in 1990.

The Snitch System, 1969- Omaha is Infiltrated

Outsiders knew of black courage and conviction and they feared it. And they feared it even more as the 1950s civil rights struggles evolved slow into more confrontative tactics. In Omaha, much of that fire was focused on fair housing. But there is little doubt that the Omaha black community was a force to be reckoned with.

The following editorial appeared on the front page of the February 5, 1960 issue of the Star under the headline, "Agitation …" Following is an excerpt:

> ***Lately some whites and some Negroes (who should know better) have counseled a go slow approach*** with regard to the many assaults on the rights of Omaha's Negro citizens. Main target of this kind of criticism is the DePorres Club. Some are saying that it has "set progress

back" because of its picketing of the Omaha School Administration. These hand wringing do-gooders and some who style themselves outspoken leaders want this paper and the DePorres Club ***to adopt a head-bowed, hat-in-hand method of commenting on the daily instances of wrong done to Negroes.***

This paper is told to ***speak more softly*** until "Things can be worked out." We say NO to such suggestions. We stand solidly behind the DePorres Club and its fighting program for arousing the conscience of the people of Omaha to correct the social injustice against the Negro people. Let there be no doubt that we will not shrink from our duty to speak out for those ***oppressed citizens…*** (p. 1—emphasis added).

A "go slow approach" being promoted by Negroes then, and the same approach is being promoted today, some 66 years later. While more than a few ministers engage in homosexual behavior and then flaunt it publicly, while at least one black political figure (Chris Rodgers) gets a $30,000 donation from Mayor Fahey so he can beat out more community-oriented competition, while an organization that claims to be about community development surreptitiously hires and then fires a young black man after ripping off his five-year vision, and while a so-called "leadership roundtable" reads about violence in the hood and then shakes and shivers like a Chihuahua trying to shit out a peach seed, this entire community here in 2004 is being told to "***go slow.***"

Omaha's black community has always had toms, opportunists, snitches and assimilationists. But in THOSE days at least, this type of negro was apparently in the minority. Let's take a trip down memory lane while I show that the numbers of sellouts, since that time, has increased exponentially.

During the late 1960s, a number of black organizations were being spied on by the federal government, a fact that is now a matter of public record. The Omaha Black Panther Party was in a building at 24th and Charles, the hub of the community. The area was still viable and vibrant, and the storefront was right across the street from the Logan-Fontenelle housing projects. The Panthers would be in the headquarters, in uniform and young people who looked up to them hung around outside. Police cars were passing through the area on a regular basis.

In the late 1960s, Jericho Honore had been trying to set up a meeting with activist David Rice, a key member of the Omaha Black Panther Party.

Some now contend that Honore, who was also the leader of a student movement on campus which led to a mass arrest – known now as the "Omaha 54" – was a snitch for the government, and that Honore was working for law enforcement officials both during his meeting with Rice and in his campus activities.

At any rate, the Omaha 54, students who were led – by Honore – to sit in at UNO Chancellor Kirk Naylor's office, were all found guilty. From there, Honore somehow became a staff writer for the Omaha Star newspaper. On May 14, 1969, an article by Honore appeared on the front page, with his picture. An edited version of the article, titled, "County Jail a Death Trap," appears below:

> Five days and four nights in the county jail are enough to kill … Conditions are such that subjection to more than "over-night" should be classified as cruel and unusual punishment.
>
> From the scum covered floors to the bug infested bunks, the crowded communal of each tank provides a festering place for disease which could become epidemic overnight.
>
> The shower stall feeds its scummy water to the middle of each 35 man tank. Many men sit to eat their meals and lay on this floor during the crowded days since there is nothing else to do.
>
> During my five days in jail, the food services amounted to tasteless garbage on a tin pan shoved at me through the bars. I took note of the following meals: Thursday – white beans and apple butter; Friday – Spanish rice and prunes; Saturday – vegetarian stew and beets. The next meal was a surprise: one thin slice of baloney with potatoes and peas.
>
> After living in filth, most prisoners seldom washed their hands before eating. They, as I, felt the filth so completely encompassing that washing seemed a waste of time …
>
> There seemed no apparent procedure for the grouping of prisoners by severity of crime. Brother Donald B., age 18, was picked up for a 1968 traffic violation and locked nightly in the cell with a white man arrested for raping an 11-year old girl. Minor offenders and murderers are thrown together.
>
> Ed Cruz (who permitted the use of his name) has spent the past 11 months awaiting the final disposition on his charge of unauthorized use of a credit card. The

> judge refused to give him credit for the time he has served.
>
> Through the prison grapevine, one of the young inmates who died in a recent fire had been sexually attacked the day before. Several admit that unnatural sexual activity is commonplace in the County Jail ...
>
> Most people have a misconception that a normal procedure exists for the 15-minute-a-week visiting privilege. But, the prisoner is separated from the visitor by double walls of closely woven heavy steel mesh which is spaced about two feet apart. The prisoner stands in the dark on one side and talks through the tiny holes to his visitor. When my sister visited, she admitted she could not see me well enough to even identify me until I spoke.
>
> Prison rules prevented her leaving cigarettes, soap or a change of underwear and socks. The only thing she could have was money from which to make purchases through the prison store with its inflated prices and irregular service. If nobody brings money, the prisoner goes without basic needs.
>
> The prison refused to allow me to bring my school books into the cell. After I asked 12 different uniformed guard personnel a total of 37 separate times for the use of these books, it was not until I complained to the Chaplain, some four days later, that they allowed me a few hours to study ....

Coincidentally, on June 11, 1969, an article appeared in the Omaha World Herald under the headline, "FBI, Police Now Zeroing in on Panthers?" Although posed as a question in the Omaha paper the article came from the Chicago Daily News Service and, as can be expected, was aimed at providing local police departments with news that they were being supported and, at the same time, to let the militant groups know that they were going to be the focus of law enforcement.

Take note of the slant of the article:

> The Black Panther Party appeared ... to be the target of a growing campaign to cripple its operation in major cities. There were indications that the campaign is being directed from the Justice Department in Washington. Within the last week, local police and agents of the Federal Bureau of Investigation have cooperated in raids on Black Panther headquarters in Chicago, Denver, and Salt Lake City. During the last several months, similar raids have been

made against Panthers in a half dozen other cities, including Des Moines, Ia. ... (Zochert, 1969: 86).

Continuing:

> A week ago, Justice Department officials declined to comment on a charge by Panther leader Bobby Seale that raids on Panther offices had been ordered by President Nixon and directed by the FBI. Tuesday, a Justice Department spokesman told the Daily News that there had been concerted 'FBI activity and investigation' with regard to the Black Panthers. He described the militant group as 'a threat to the internal security of the country' (Zochert, 1969: 86).

On June 26, 1969 – two days after Vivian Strong was killed by the Omaha police officer – the national campaign against the Black Panther Party continued to find a home in Omaha, Nebraska. A group calling itself the Support Your Local Police Committee which was admittedly in the process of becoming a committee of the John Birch Society (according to Richard Beem, coordinator for the Society), brought in Alan Stang, a speaker out of New York. Stang, whose articles had appeared in publications such as American Opinion and Review of the News, said that a large number of attacks on policemen across the country during the previous 18 months could be traced to an organized campaign by the Black Panther Party (Omaha World Herald, 1969: 4).

The day of the speech, which was given at Bryan Junior High School, Beem called a press conference and told those in attendance that many policemen had been shot from ambush in an effort "to destroy the fabric of government."

In January of 1970 – six months after the previous article appeared, and the same year that David Rice and Ed Poindexter were "railroaded" by the Omaha Police Division, two other members of the Black Panther Party were also attacked – literally. An article that appeared on January 8, 1970, to the Omaha Star, written by Rice, shows what happened to Frank and Will Peak:

> On Friday, January 2nd, Frank, Will and Duane Peak were selling Black Panther papers at Caniglia's Drive-In at 30th and Fort. At approximately 10:40 pm, Timothy Murtaugh and a few companions began shouting racist

epithets at the Peaks and and threatening them with physical harm. Frank, Will and Duane tried in vain to relate to Murtaugh and companions (all white) on an ideological and verbal level. But their words were met by further racist epithets and finally, violence.

With utter quickness, a group of over 20 whites jumped out of cars and joined Murtaugh, Swenson, and others in a brutal attack upon the three Panther paper selling Blacks. Being greatly outnumbered, Frank and Will Peak reached into their car, which was parked close at hand, and grabbed their pistols.

The three Black men fought off the large crowd of whites for about ten minutes, with the assistance of two pistol handles. Finally, Will and Duane broke loose, jumped in their car, and made it to a public phone at twenty-fourth and Fort. Frank fought on desperately to survive but eventually fell to the ground, where he was repeatedly kicked and stomped all over his body. Soon afterwards, members of the Omaha Police Department arrived on the scene. Upon their arrival the whites moved away from Frank. And the police promptly arrested him.

In the meantime the police discovered Will and Duane walking at 24th and Fort, toward their car. One of the police pointed his gun at them and ordered them to stop at the car. By this time about four cruisers gathered.

The police got out of their cruisers and grabbed Will and Duane, placed handcuffs on them, and separated the two. While one group of police beat Duane on one side of the street, the other group dealt with Will: one police kept ordering Will to become further spread against the car, until he finally fell to the ground. When he hit the ground, only one of his hands having been cuffed, they cuffed his other hand. Then they pistol-whipped him about the head and face, clubbed him, and kicked him about the head and sides. And to add frosting to the cake, they held him down and bent his legs to the point of tearing muscles in one leg so that he was thereafter unable to walk.
By David L. Rice
Deputy Minister of Information

The Black Panther Party dominated the headlines, both locally and nationally. In May of 1970, Huey Newton, co-founder and Minister of Defense of the Black Panther Party, was denied parole by the California Adult Authority in San Luis Obispo, California (Omaha Star, 1970: 1).

In the summer of 1970, a phone call is made to the Omaha police department and the caller says that a woman is being raped. An address is given and two police officers respond. One of the officers, Larry Minard, enters the house with his colleague and picks up a suitcase which triggers a bomb. Minard is blown to bits. Rudy Smith covered the story as a photographer for the Omaha World Herald.

The fire squad and police squad were already there when Smith arrived. He recalls that the house was sitting on a hill, and there was a great deal of pandemonium, shouting and screaming by the police department. Black bystanders were ushered out of the area to the end of the street and the police refused to let anyone come up the hill.

Out of all that, two Black Panther members, David Rice and Ed Poindexter, were arrested, tried and convicted of first-degree murder. All of this was based on the testimony of a teen aged youth, Duane Peak, who appeared in court badly beaten and afraid. According to Smith, the Omaha chapter of the Black Panther Party was dropped from the national organization for reasons "that were not clear." Frank T. Peak, long-time community activist and cousin of Duane, feels that it had something to do with a difference in the perspectives of Midwest and California members. There is also evidence, however, that the breaking away from the national chapter by the Midwest chapter may have been the results of undercover police work, as part of the FBI's COINTELPRO ("Counterintelligence Program).

Following the death of Officer Minard, on August 20, 1970, the Omaha Star carried a front page story titled, "Police-Community Problems Can Be Solved by 'Committed Action,'" and summed up the views shared at a "forum" which has been held at the First Central Congregational Church. Some segments of the press and the police had complained because the police were not invited to attend the forum.

In response to the forum, Police Captain William Pattavina said, "All these policemen ever get are preachers talking about police brutality. They never want to hear our side of it. Ask those preachers what they're going to do about the five orphans (the children of Patrolman Minard) (Omaha Star, 1970: 1). A prepared statement was delivered by four of the five sponsors of the forum including the Rev. James D. Hargleroad, director of the Omaha Presbytery's Commission on Church and Race; The Rev. Jerry Elrod, director of the United Methodist Metropolitan Ministries; the Rev. Victor R. Schoonover of the Greater Omaha Area Lutherans; and Harold Adler, director of the Anti-Defamation League. The fifth sponsor, Rev. Jerry

Burbach, director of Catholic Social Action was out of the city and did not sign the prepared statement.

Following is the full text of that statement:

> Innocent victims are frequently caught in tragic human misunderstandings and injustices. Such was the unfortunate case in the early Monday morning bombing incident which took the life of Patrolman Larry Minard.
>
> Sponsors of Friday's Forum, during which statements of police community relations matters were made by local citizens, express their deep regret and sympathy at the tragic loss of life connected with Monday night's bombing. As in the death of Vivian Strong, one year ago, we deplore such waste of human life.
>
> The Forum was an initial means for calling attention to the seriousness of the widening gap between much of the Omaha community and the Police Department. When such seriousness is recognized, positive action for overcoming that gap may then develop.
>
> Further, the organizers of the Forum, along with a number of the ministers present, were anxious that since moral questions are at issue, the religious community of Omaha be made aware of those issues and bring its influence to correct them in behalf of all citizens.
>
> Part of Friday's Forum allowed participants the chance to hear, in detail, an issue into frequently given public airing. Such forums on a wide variety of community issues have been sponsored by some organizing group in the past.
>
> The Forum was designed to create positive citizen concern in dealing with present police-community misunderstandings.
>
> The sponsors of the first Forum are anxious that a similar opportunity be made available to explore both present and past tensions between the community and police. Such an effort cooperative in its intent, could result in positive strides toward needed improved relations between the community and the police, a goal of many.
>
> The regret and sympathy of some of the retaliatory attitude of others combined will not solve the present tensions in Omaha. Committed attention to that tension and their causes coupled with disciplined energy to solve them will.

First of all, the bullshit just said about Larry Minard is the exactly crap that was said about Jimmy Wilson Jr. and more recently Jason Pratt. The regrets expressed are not universal; Omaha is segregated by residence and race. It is also segregated in terms of the quality of treatment that residents get from the cops. The white folks see the rosy-colored Larry Minard, the whimsical Jimmy Wilson and the pristine and practical Jason Pratt. Black people – whose community these white boys patrol – see them as they really are, stripped of their pomp and impious ceremony. We see one thing: **crackers!**

The preceding excerpt made the claim: *"The Forum was an initial means for calling attention to the seriousness of the widening gap between much of the Omaha community and the Police Department. When such seriousness is recognized, positive action for overcoming that gap may then develop."* So in other words, it was clearly NOT recognized because the relationship has grown WORSE over the years, not better.

Forums and talk. And then when it's over, another black man gets croaked. Why? Because there are those of us who are feeding information to the police and the police, in turn, are using that information as a reason to destroy us, one by one. Want proof?

1981 – Omaha and "Mr. Snitch"

On September 28, 1981, the Omaha Police Division botched a "raid" on public housing, more specifically the Hilltop Homes. What was the raid based on: information from a confidential informant known as "Mr. Snitch." Senator Ernie Chambers provided the following overview and explanation:

PETITION ON POLICE BRUTALITY 9-29-81

There was a Bible meeting at 2441 North 33rd Street at approximately 7:15 p.m., at about 7:30 or 7:35, a neighbor ran into the house along with two youngsters terribly frightened. The lady was so horrified she ran under the kitchen table and turned it over while hitting her head on it. We didn't know what was going on. The police started shooting and everyone was terrified. Everyone was running around in the house while the police were steadily shooting out windows, cussing at us, and calling us dirty names and "Niggers". They put handcuffs on innocent people, made us lie down on the ground and kneed us in our backs. Some had bruises and cuts. They really treated us like animals. We were really treated bad, as though we were uncivilized cannibals. They could have killed children and innocent people. All they said for the situation was "I'm sorry, that's the breaks." So sign this petition and we will turn it over to Ernie Chambers, Mike Adams and Fred Connelly. Something needs to be done. Don't let this happen again, without trying to help cease this brutality.

The incident took place on the evening of Monday, September 28, 1981. The Omaha World Herald reported that a crowd of *"several hundred people gathered after the shooting, shouting racial slurs and foul comments at police."* (World Herald 9-28-81, morning edition)

As the facts of the situation unfold, it will become clear why the people directed hostile comments against the police ...

For the sake of coherence and to provide a point of reference, a brief summary will be presented, following in the main, the "official" version given by police officials, acquiesced in by Mayor Mike Boyle and published by the World-Herald. Discrepancies, contradictions, distortions and suppressed information will be dealt with later.

Two cases are being inserted here to demonstrate that: 1) the incident could have been handled successfully without a massive show of force or danger or injury to anyone; and, 2) when White persons are involved, the police tend to exercise far more restraint.

CASE No. 1   About three years ago, the Bristol Market was held up by armed gunmen who fired a shot inside the store. They fled about a block north into the Spencer Homes Public Housing Project (OHA) and took refuge in one of the apartments. Some residents knew what had happened and where the men had gone.

Officers Marvin McClarty, James Patterson, Michael Crocker (all Black) and Lt. Goodman (White) arrived. There was no flooding of the area with police vehicles nor a show of armed force. One of the residents who knew the officers, approached them and told them he had marked the apartment contained by the men by placing a green cup on the front porch. Arrests were made without incident, as the men offered no resistance. The money and guns were recovered.

CASE No. 2   This case is presented through the attached article which reveals that, even though the officers met with actual violent resistance and physical interference, no one was shot at or injured -- and only TWO arrests were made. All the persons were White.

COMPARE THIS WITH THKE BRUTAL HANDLING OF INNOCENT WOMEN AND CHILDREN IN A HOUSING COMPLEX -- NOT A TAVERN. VIOLENTLY-RESISTING WHITE TAVERN PATRONS FACED LESS POLICE VIOLENCE THAN DID INNOCENT BLACK PEOPLE AT <u>BIBLE</u> STUDY!

SUMMARY

Pursuant to information from "Mr. Snitch," police knew that two men suspected of involvement in several robberies were at 2437 North 33rd Street. The apartment is located at the very end (south) end of a 5-plex and is conspicuous because of a large letter "K" painted on its bricks.

Two teams of plainclothes officers were formed. One consisted of: (1) Charles Prokupek, (2) Thomas Gorgen. The other: (1) Alan Abbott (shot by Officer Briese), (2) Paul Briese (shot Officer Abbott), (3) Frank O'Connor (fired a shotgun into the wrong apartment), (4) Richard Swircinski (put a tourniquet on Officer Abbott).

They arrived at the scene in an unmarked black Chevy van and parked at the rear of <u>2437</u> North 33rd Street. (Significant conflicts in accounts which occur after this point will be considered in detail later.)

According to the "official" version, *"Swircinski <u>entered</u> the rear door of 2437 North 33rd Street."* Abbott and O'Connor *"were moving to assist"* him when they *"attempted to <u>stop</u> two black <u>males</u> for questioning and identification."* The two *"<u>broke away</u> and ran to the rear door of <u>2439</u> North 33rd Street with the officers in pursuit."*

According to the "official" version, the two black males ran through the apartment and out the front door. Abbott emerged behind them with his shotgun. Briese, positioned at the front of the building, *"ordered (Abbott) to halt"*. Abbott *"in a crouched position"*, turned toward Briese who claimed not to be able to recognize him in the darkness. Thinking Abbott was a *"suspect"*, Briese said he fired one blast from his riot gun, striking Abbott in the right arm.

O'Connor then emerged. He, thinking that whoever shot Abbott had run inside the next door apartment (2441 North 33rd Street), fired a blast from his riot gun through the living room window and a second blast through an unoccupied upstairs bedroom window. No one was hit.

In the meantime, the <u>occupants</u> of 2439 (Margaret and Kenneth Perry, Anna Tolbert and Faye Perry) fled in terror from the white gunmen who had invaded their apartment.

Noteworthy is the fact that the two persons who exited the front door ahead of Abbott and O'Connor were Anna Tolbert and Faye Perry -- <u>not</u> *"two black males"* -- and both were <u>already inside</u> 2439 when Abbott and O'Connor invaded.

Margaret and Kenneth Perry ran out the <u>back</u> door as Abbott and O'Connor chased Anna Tolbert and Faye Perry out the front. Margaret entered the back door of <u>2441</u> followed by Kenneth. Margaret sought refuge under the table, turning it over. Kenneth was too frightened to speak to the startled women seated around the table having Bible study.

When the living room window was shattered by O'Connor's first blast, everyone scattered and headed upstairs. A second blast went through thke window of an unoccupied bedroom. Thinking the invading white gunmen were members of the KU KLUX KLAN, someone cried, "Call the police!" Another person who had looked out the window and seen cruisers, responded, "That <u>is</u> the police!"

They heard a man (O'Connor) yelling somebody's name and ordering him to come out. Thinking the name was Kenny Perry, they began pressuring Kenneth to go outside so that "all of us won't be killed!" Someone (Officer West) began pounding on the front door, ordering everyone to "come out or we will come in and get you."

Though terrified at the prospect of being shot to death, Kenneth Perry under the insistent urging of the others, *crawled down the stairs* and outside where he was grabbed, forced through some bushes and into a cruiser. The others filed out and were forced to lie spread-eagle face down on the ground. Cocked shotguns were placed near the head of some of them; they were cursed, handcuffed, taken to jail and held several hours and questioned before being released without charge ...

And Omaha Police Division (OPD) Internal Security Investigation apparently concluded that <u>no OPD policies, procedures or regulations were violated. No disciplinary action was imposed on any officer.</u>

September 29, 1981, the day after the incident, Acting Police Chief Keith Lant issued a press release, containing <u>falsification</u> and distortion of purported "facts", <u>misrepresentations</u> regarding the sequence of events and <u>suppression</u> of important facts. The text of the press release:

Officer Alan J. Abbott, thirty-seven years of age, was accidentally shot and severely wounded in the right forearm while attempting to serve a felony arrest warrant at 2437 North 33rd Street at approximately 7:30 p.m. on Monday, 28 September 1981.

Officer Abbott was accidentally wounded by another member of the four man arrest team, Officer Paul Briese. Both officers are currently assigned to the Robbery/Sex Unit of the Criminal Investigation Bureau.

The suspect named in the felony warrant was Roy Ellis, black male, twenty-seven years of age, wanted for the attempted robbery of Commercial Federal Savings and Loan at 36th and "q" which occurred on 9 September 1981. This attempted robbery also involved an abduction and auto theft. The Police Officers involved in the arrest team had reliable information tha the suspect was in the end unit of a five-plex at 2437 North 33rd Street. They pulled up to the rear of the unit and Officer Briese took a position in front of 2437 North 33rd Street to cover the front door. Officer Richard Swircinski <u>entered the rear door</u> of 2437 North 33rd Street. The other two officers, Frank O'Connor and Alan Abbott, at that time <u>were moving to assist</u> Officer Swircinski but <u>attempted to stop two black males</u> at the rear of the unit for questioning and identification. These two parties <u>broke away and ran to the rear door of 2439</u> North 33rd Street with the <u>officers in pursuit</u>. The <u>two suspects exited the front door</u> and were ordered to halt by Officer Briese. <u>They</u> continued to run north along the front of the five-plex. At that time, Officer Abbott existed the front of 2439 North 33rd Street <u>in a crouched position</u> carrying a police riot gun. In the darkness, Officer Briese believed Officer Abbott to be <u>an armed suspect</u> and <u>ordered him to halt.</u> At this time, Officer Abbott turned, still in a crouched position, to face Officer Briese. Officer Briese fired the police riot gun hitting Officer Abbott in the right forearm. A "Help an Officer" call was put out and other officers arrived on the scene. Two arrests were then made at 2437 North 33rd Street: Roy Ellis and Harold Davis, also wanted for robbery. They were taken into custody in the upstairs area of 2437 North 33rd Street. Both suspects have been booked into Central Detention for robbery charges (Emphasis added-- E.C.)

Lant misstated facts in a number of particulars and suppressed completely, the most important fact of all:

Officer Briese, after having shot Abbott, lied to O'Connor, telling him that someone else had shot Abbot and had run into the apartment at 2441.

The lie is especially reprehensible and vicious because it turned O'Connor (according to the statements of witnesses) into a virtual madman and sent him on a shooting spree into an apartment occupied by innocent women and children, recklessly <u>endangering their lives</u>....

... In addition to that, Briese's lie set in motion a chain of near-fatal events which included the transmission of an erroneous radio message that led other officers to believe that an officer had been broght down by "barricaded gunmen." When these misinformed officers arrived on the scene, they took cover behind cruisers, trees and buildings -- and produced guns of various kinds, creating a great hazard.

The World Herald repeatedly printed the lie in several editions and never corrected it.

This took place 23 years ago. But it should show how little has changed over those two decades. These cops are still "mishandling" situations in North Omaha, and they are still getting away with it. Want proof?

1982 – Crime Prevention as Aide to Revitalition

Meanwhile, in March of 1982 Richard Wadman was sworn in as Omaha's 22nd permanent police chief. Wadman was deputy public safety commissioner of Utah since 1978 and before that he was chief of police of Orem, Utah, a town with no black residents. While deputy public safety commissioner, he lived in Orem. He was also a member of the West Covina, California Police Department for two years, *a special agent for the Drug Enforcement Agency* for three years and a San Diego, California patrolman for seven years. Wadman was born and raised in San Diego. (Travis, 1982: 1)

No sooner was he in office than Wadman assembled a team of 12 officers and a civilian employee. The team was headed by Captain John Mitchell and was directed to ***find ways to improve public relations***. One recommendation was called "District Awareness," with the idea of officers spending more time outside their cruisers and getting to know people better in the districts they served. Beat patrols were expanded and officers in cruisers were instructed to learn all they could about the residents of a district and the trouble spots. (Omaha World Herald, 1982: 18)

In his first speech as police chief, Wadman claimed he would guide the Omaha Police Department toward an emphasis of snuffing crime before it happens. "The bottom line of effective police work is the absence of crime," Wadman said. (Krajicek, 1982: 8)

But Omaha, for the most part, has very little crime. According to the Uniform Crime Reports from 1993, Omaha ranked 7th in cities with populations from 250,000 to 500,000 in offenses known to police. The only cities ahead of Omaha were (1) Virginia Beach, VA; (2) Louisville, KY; (3) Anchorage, AK; (4) Colorado Springs, CO.; (5) Santa Ana, CA.; and (6) Arlington, TX. (Omaha Police Department, 1994: 20)

For cities of comparable size, Omaha ranked number TWO in the nation in 1993 in lowest crime. The only city ahead of it was Colorado Springs, Colorado. (Omaha Police Department, 1994: 13)

But you have to report crime and pretend that you have problems if you want to continue to rake in those Federal grant dollars (free money). And that is where North Omaha comes in.

What little crime there is in and around North Omaha are, by and large, the kinds of crimes that low-income people commit (robberies, turning on one another, etc,) I would be willing to bet that less than one percent of one percent of crime in North Omaha goes beyond the black community's borders. One article stated,

> Omaha consistently is ranked above the national average for crime clearance in virtually every category. Wadman said beefed-up prevention will complement that.
> (Krajicek, 1982: 8)

Here is why crime clearance is so high. Omaha has more "snitches per capita" than probably any city its size. And in North Omaha, unlike other black areas, the snitches can walk around and not have to worry about being attacked for snitching. Paying for information is one way that the Omaha Police Division has traditionally gotten its job done and the existence of a Police Informant Fund receives public support, as was the case in April of 1980:

> A report on the success of the Omaha Police Department's Information fund and announcement of a new donation to it are expected at an afternoon press conference today. Police sources said a representative of the Nebraska and Omaha Food Retailers Association is expected to attend, and Mayor Veys will release statistics describing how the fund has been used. Veys, a grocer, is a member of the association. In past years, the association has been the chief civilian contributor to the fund, donating at least $6,000 since 1977. (Omaha World Herald, 1980: no page number)

Furthermore,

> The association, mostly Omaha-area grocers, originally offered rewards for information leading to arrests in certain cases. But in 1977, police officials suggested that an informant fund would be more effective ... The association's first $1,500 contribution led to recovery of $35,000 worth of stolen property, police officials said. The money is used to buy information, police said. *Without it, detectives might have more difficulty obtaining information* ... (Omaha World Herald, 1980: no page--emphasis added-MCS)

But there's more. At least three of the four major TV stations have crime telecasts such as "WeTip,""Crimestoppers" and the like. Channel 7 boasts of even having a segment called "the crime beat," which features individuals considered "most wanted" from this area. Third, Omaha only has 300,000 people although they lie and claim there's more. And there are 600 officers. But that breaks down to about 5,000 people per officer. But since most of the officers are in North Omaha -- an area with about 60,000 residents -- this breaks down only 1,000 people per officer!

These cops have it easy and most of the crimes involve crimes that are the result of segregation and racism -- two elements of social disorder that they are pledged to defend and uphold! "To Protect and Serve" is what the do for white people and for property owners -- not for the blacks whom they harass, pull over, brutalize and sometimes kill.

Wadman talks of beefing up prevention, but evidently that didn't work because the best form of prevention is a JOB, and blacks were no less unemployed under Wadman than they were under any other police chief. And that is the key: keep the poor in that state because by doing so, your hick city qualifies for grants that they ordinarily would not receive. You can lie to the out of touch Federal government and promise to "help," get the money, and then turn around and spend it on your own race members!

So the city power brokers maintain poverty and the police therefore continue to have jobs patrolling the impoverished area.

Also in March, a group calling itself North Omaha Community Development enlisted the help of the police to discuss ways to revitalize North Omaha. It was the usual "all talk, no action" scam, but Omahans didn't know that at the time. But an article documenting the "study," as it was called, did include some very important words by then Police Chief Robert Wadman. Take note:

> Wadman said **crime enforcement is a companion to revitalization;** 24th and Lake Streets has a bad reputation for crime, so people would be reluctant to locate a business there. Wadman said statistics may show that the area is not a hotbed of crime most people think. **He said the fear of crime may be more substantial than actual incidents of crime. (Omaha World Herald, 1982: 4— emphasis added)**

By June of 1982, Wadman was on his way to establishing a reputation for "being aggressive." This aggressiveness was reflected in the fact that in June of 1981, only three months after he assumed office, it was reported that Omaha area law enforcement officials remained among the nation's top users of telephone wiretaps on suspected criminals, and Wadman vowed that "wiretaps will continue to be used aggressively in Omaha." (Williams, 1982: 6)

But "listening in" was not only a matter of police policy, evidently. As far back as June of 1978, State Senator Ernie Chambers complained about eavesdropping telephone operators for Northwestern Bell who he said were listening in on his collect and credit card calls. The issue was so serious that there were several meetings and letters exchanged between Chambers and Northwestern Bell executives. (Omaha World Herald, 1978)

In June of 1982, the results of a 16 month study of relations between Omaha police and blacks was made public by spokesmen for the group responsible -- the Nebraska Advisory Committee to the U.S. Commission on Civil Rights. The Commission recommended that changes be made in 10 areas, some of which then Police Chief Robert Wadman said were already underway:

> Among the committee recommendations that have already been announced by Wadman are changes in recruiting and training of minority officers (a major issue since the city signed a U.S. Justice Department consent decree deeming that 40 percent of police recruit classes be black); increased contact with citizens through foot patrols; expansion of community relations programs, and human relations training for both recruits and experienced officers. (Krajicek, 1982: 4)

Charles Washington, a member of the Advisory Committee, said at the time that for him, a close look into the process by which citizens can make complaints of police misconduct was a key element of the report. But Charlie also knew that along with Cornelius Gaines, I had been working on a Police-Civilian Review Board which would have subpoena power. However, both Mayor Al Veys and later, Mike Boyle when he was elected, both opposed the idea for a review board.

On August 8, 1982 former Police Chief Richard Andersen died at Clarkson Hospital, where he had been hospitalized for several weeks. He was 58 and the cause of death was cancer. Andersen directed the police department for nearly 14 years -- from August 5, 1967 to May 21, 1981. That was longer than any other chief in the city's history. In order to put Omaha crime figures in perspective, Andersen instituted a regular comparative analysis of crimes in cities of similar population, which generally showed Omaha to have less violence. Andersen refused to take credit or blame for crime rate increases or decreases, saying he believed crime rates were cyclical and independent of police work. (Omaha World Herald, 1982: 1; King & Fogarty, 1980: 3)

One can cogently contend that were it not for the racist patrolling of North Omaha, the police in Omaha would not have anything to do. When they need more officers (or want them when there is no need), the excuse is somewhere to be found in the black community. The request for more officers generates a debate for more money and, after all, that is what "crime fighting" is all about: money and manpower. So they go about scaring the public by pretending that they are somehow "undermanned" and then they come up with statistics which are aimed at scaring the white suburban voter and before you know it they have the money to further repress the black community.

An example of this can be found in a statement made by then-Police Chief Richard Andersen in February of 1980:

> Statistics released Thursday indicated serious crime in Omaha in 1979 was up 13 percent over 1978. Andersen said police are particularly busy in the area north of Bedford Avenue and east of 72nd Street, largely because of an increase in crime ... (McCoy, 1980)

The area described above is north Omaha. *And it is the same area that they now use some 17 years later to justify Weed and Seed grants and other programs aimed at arresting young black males.* And the reason why that area has remained poor is by design; it is the 68111 zip code that brings in the lion's share of Federal money that pays for police overtime, among other things!

1989 – The Rise of "Mad Dads"

From time to time a number of organizations have arisen to champion the cause of North Omaha: the DePorres Club, the 4CL, Mothers for Adequate Welfare, the Survival Coalition, the Coalition Against Injustice, and the Triple One organizations, just to name a few. During that same time other groups that came into fruition did the system's bidding: those include, but are not limited to, North Omaha Community Development, MAD DADS, the Omaha Small Business Network and others – who will be named at another time and place.

None of them were as duplicitous as the group calling itself the MAD DADS.

EDDIE STATON, MAD DADS AND THEWORLD HERALD ARTICLE: "Show Him the Money!!"

By Matthew C. Stelly, blackomahaonline analyst

The World Herald and its writers have, over the years, proven to be our bitter enemies. They prop up those who would do black people harm while, at the same time, pummeling those who are working in our defense and development. A case in point appeared in the Sunday, July 11th edition of the paper under the headline, "Mad Dads Founder Sees Much To Be Mad About in the Black Community."

Like A'Jamal Byndon (Catholic Charities) and Bill Cosby who only writes articles and make public statements that let white folks off the hook and degrade black people as a group, Staton has always been called upon by white folks to "explain things" to the black community. Some of us have short memories and this is why Staton was able to come back to Omaha for a staged interview with the World-Herald, and reporter Julia McCord, who just so happened to be at the Omaha Press Club while Staton was glaring out of the window.

This essay is aimed at refuting the fluff piece that the World-Herald distributed on Sunday and to offer clarity where ideological confusion apparently reigns. Following are some "facts" that the most racist newspaper in the Midwest forgot to add. First, to recap.

In 1989 a group was formed after the son of John Foster was killed by gangs. The group called itself MAD DADS, an acronym that stands for Men Against Destruction and Defending Against Drugs and Disorder. They might have been in line with the first part of that name, but there is no doubt that since their formation, both drugs and disorder increased and, in fact, one of the so-called founders – Eddie Staton – has had relatives hooked on drugs and, in fact, his own WIFE was a hooked on crack cocaine. But this is but the tip of the iceberg when it comes to the rise to power of this now nationally recognized organization.

The fact is, if you wanted to cop drugs, young people went straight to the parking lot of the so-called "headquarters" of Mad Dads. They did nothing about it. When a grant was available for part of a "gun buyback" program, there was the Mad Dads, getting paid to disarm the black community.

The organization's logo shows an outstretched white hand covered by a black fist. Robert Tyler, at the time the group's treasurer and a minister described the logo as showing "the hand of reasoning and the fist of determination" being viewed as one. Both were missing noticeably as the months turned into years, and the Mad Dads became more concerned about looking good, making money and getting headlines than they were about doing anything credible in North Omaha's black community.

The group went from two offices in Omaha, one at 3030 Sprague Street and the other at 3309-1/2 North 30th Street to a decision to move to Florida. Why? To follow the money, of course.

Did the MAD DADS make an impact in Omaha? In at least one area they did: the area of "training" being provided to "interested communities" in areas around the nation. For instance, in 1990, then-President George Bush came to Omaha and presented the group with his "Thousand Points of Light Award" for volunteerism, and the following year, co-founder John Foster went to Los Angeles to meet with community leaders there and spread the ideas of the MAD DADS concept. During that time there was even talk of opening up a chapter there, and eventually, one was developed.

In 1992, then mayor of New York David Dinkins came to Omaha (translation: junket) to "look at the group's techniques," and then in 1993, the MAD DADS went on a junket to the Big Apple. There is also a group that was formed in nearby Council Bluffs, Iowa, where businessman Rick Gilland used video cameras to record crime.

But on the other hand, what about the actual purpose of the group? What did they do that made an impact upon neutralizing the growth of gang-related criminal activity? Nothing. But they did make a lot of friends with the police, with perhaps the most racist mayor that Omaha ever had (Hal Daub) and when called upon, Staton was always ready with some kind of mealy-mouthed explanation that would make white folks feel good and put blame squarely upon the backs of blacks.

One may recall the machismo-laden words of the organizers, and in particular, John Foster, who said during the nascent stages of the organization's development, that, "We decided to start the group because we're tired of the complacency of black men in our community." He continued: "I'm pointing the finger at myself as well. We are to blame for many of the things that have been happening in the community, and its time for us to stand up and say we are tired of being tired. We are tired of the drugs and gang violence. We need to set an example for our kids ..."

John was a serious brother and although he has passed, this writer believes he was a lot more serious about the organization than Staton.

Now, let us look at the facts.

First of all, what really ended up happening was that the Mad Dads wanted to set an example of how to get PAID for working in the community. Because, as you will see as this story unfolds, that appears to have been the aim, intent and purpose of Staton all along. But there are other facts worthy of consideration.

During the heyday and hijinks of the Mad Dads, then-Police Sergeant William Muldoon, said that drug-related crimes "have remained fairly constant over the past four years."

There is nothing "constant" about a rise is possession of controlled substances (an increase of almost 400 cases over a 2 year period in a city as small as Omaha's). This constitutes a rise in crime that flies in the face of the following facts: (1) most of the police cruisers are located in the black community where a disproportionate number of these "busts" take place; (2) Omaha's "crime wave" is mild compared with cities of comparable size (Milwaukee, Indianapolis); (3) the fact that Omaha is segregated which makes "patrolling the minorities" all the more easier since most are concentrated either on the north side (African-Americans) or the south side (Latinos) and (4) the fact that the local media, from the major newspaper to all four television stations, assist the police not only through community service programs such as "Crime Stoppers," but more importantly through biased reporting (relying almost solely on the police side of the story) which, in turn, justifies the need for more police, more overtime, increases in play, and the like. In fact, Omaha has been voted one of the "best dressed police departments" in the nation.

And of course, the 'crime-fighting' Mad Dads, right?

Now, to answer the question about the MAD DADS, who received more than their share of grant money to "fight crime" and deal with gangs. This is the central point: John Foster at one time spoke about being "tired of being tired." But it is strange that the group went from "concerned fathers" to seeking to get PAID for what they did. The fact of the matter is, the impact of gangs increased since the advent of the MAD DADS and, as we saw earlier, the rise in the use of controlled substances also increased. Black teen homicides also increased. And what the group ended up offering after its on-going failures to make a dent in crime, was to begin snitching on black kids and turning them in to the cops!

Furthermore, elsewhere I document that former police Chief Robert Wadman was instrumental in not only allowing the Bloods and the Crips to set up shop in Omaha, but also played a role in the proliferation of drugs saturating the area. At any rate these crack dealers have the money to make bail and are detained for a short time, then released after the police get information on who their supplier is. After this, the police work their way up the chain and find out who "Mr. Big" is – but they don't take action on what they know. It is in the best interests of those in power to keep minorities on drugs, high and confused. In that way they cannot rebel against a government that oppresses them. Furthermore, the drug industry is now big business and, when one combines it with the prison construction business, billions are generated for the system and jobs for whites in small towns, where these prisons are located, can keep the economy booming.

Moreover, we must remember that the Near North Side is no more than ten square miles in diameter, with the heart of it being an approximately 8-square mile area. This means that thanks to segregation, population density and of course racism, the Omaha Police Department should well know who the drug abusers in the area are, who the drug dealers are and where the crimes that are drug-related are being committed. And so should the allegedly "street-wise" Mad Dads.

Finally, we add in the variable of conspicuous consumption. This translates in this particular case to mean that drug dealers want to be recognized by those they live around; they want to be flashy in a community that is low in self-esteem. Therefore, the customized cars, the vanity license plates, the fancy clothes and jewelry all enable these people to stand out in a community where far too many people don't even have jobs. Generally then, because of employment discrimination, a black male with a foreign car and gold rings on is going to be most likely involved in some kind of "underground activity," according to the logic of the police. That is the way that Omaha has "rigged" the game; and those who are successful in a legitimate way do not, for the most part, reside in the central city.

And the Mad Dads fell prey to the same kinds of conspicuous consumption: leather jackets, seeking more money, vans and the like. They became as consumed with "things" as the drug dealers they were formed to oppose. Who were they accountable to? The racist white police department and racist Mayor Hal Daub?

One incident shows this was the case. Following the shooting of Police Officer Jimmy Wilson Jr., there was a community meeting held at OOIC. Mayor Daub was there and Eddie Staton was there defending him. At one point Daub turned to Eddie and told him, "Enough said, Eddie." And Staton got the message.

During an "investigation" of the 1992 murder of North High student Kenyatta Bush, the MAD DADS "conducted its own searches" and got the community to contribute more than $15,000 to a "reward fund." Where is that money? How was it spent? They also claimed to be disclosing information on the progress being made so that the community could be better informed. A year later, Kenyatta's murderer was supposedly found by the police and supposedly killed himself while in custody. Furthermore, many more youth have died since that time. The question is: where is the $15,000?

When a 13-year-old girl was raped, the MAD DADS set up a reward fund and raised $500. But when a young girl was killed right on the block of the MAD DADS' headquarters, the location of the death was downplayed, and I was at the hospital the night that young sister took her last breath. Gun buybacks, tours of corrections facilities, speeches, block parties, movie screenings (such as the advanced screening of 'Boyz N' The Hood) and reward funds are important. But these are not the acts of people who are doing anything any different than existing neighborhood watch groups.

When I taught Black Studies at the University of Nebraska at Omaha, I made sure that my students wrote papers on a subject having something to do with North Omaha. Since most of those students were white, I wanted to "de-mystify" and "de-demonize" the black community; to offset the lies and myths that their parents and neighbors had concocted behind the backs of blacks.

In the final analysis, it was about the money. A suit by the Nebraska Department of Social Services over misspent grant money and an incident where the group used a helicopter to conduct nighttime searches were but two of these problems. The group received some bad press and criticism from both of them. Mad Dads is a non-profit organization. They live solely off of grants and contributions. In 1991, the Nebraska State Department of Social Services gave the group a grant of $50,000. $20,000 of that money was to be used to start a surrogate parent program in North Omaha.

But they continued to turn in young black males. Then came yet another fundraising drive and an eleven-member advisory board – made up almost entirely of crackers.

Stating that the MAD DADS "have to be just as sophisticated to fight back" against drug dealers who have cellular phones, beepers and hand signals, the group called an August 1989 press conference and announced a computerized telephone machine that could take up to 1,000 calls a day, field incoming calls and make printouts of the information received. The $8,000 machine would enable the MAD DADS to give out information about the organization, drug use and who to contact about drug and gang problems. Now check this out: At that press conference Staton said that any information obtained could be shared with the Omaha Police Department and the Douglas County Sheriff's Office.

This group, which is supposed to consist of "role models" should, you would think, be able to manage its own money, its own business and be a leader in making decisions for and in the community, right? No. These individuals, in addition to falling prey to tendencies of conspicuous consumption, are also guilty of the same "beg and borrow" two fold economy that a number of low-income persons practice. Not only that, but recall that a "management team" had to be brought in to watch and make sure that these grown men didn't "abuse" any of the funds.

Now the group has ordered a computerized telephone system and, it appeared, didn't even have a way to pay for it. According to the World-Herald, officials of Mad Dads were asking for donations to help pay for the equipment, which was purchased from Faxtel Ltd. of Omaha. Mort Sullivan, president of Faxtel, demonstrated the equipment Tuesday and said it could 'help mobilize an army.' "We're talking about a lot of firepower that no one else in the nation has," Sullivan said. "I hope (the drug dealers) know we're coming."

Was the community consulted about the machine prior to it being ordered by the MAD DADS? Was the community involved in the selection process? This white man, Mort Sullivan, is none other than the same man who would put out a newspaper dogging out Abe Baker, then the owner of Baker's Supermarkets, regarding Baker's buying up of land in and around the black community. Then, I would find out later, Sullivan was just angry because Baker had beat HIM out on some attempts to do the same thing. So Sullivan, a Jew, goes up against another Jew in the name of "helping out blacks" – the same thing he appears to be doing by selling this "telephone system" to the MAD DADS. Does it surprise you that the "retirement home of the Jews" – the state of Florida – would be a place where Staton would make his home?

When originally formed, they told the community that they were seeking "strong men of all races." And now, a dozen years later, we find these same people turning in their own kids to the white man in exchange for credibility and a pat on the head. *Does it take a really strong man to betray his own child?*

Now, we are in a position to better understand the contents of the July 11, 2004 article that appeared in the World-Herald. The entire article proves, at the end of the day, that Eddie Staton has not changed one bit. Check it out:

> *Eddie Staton looked out of the Omaha Press Club's 22nd floor window on the new buildings in downtown Omaha last weekend was impressed. Qwest Center Omaha. Gallup University. Union Pacific Railroad's new headquarters. The World Herald's Freedom Center. "This is phenomenal," Staton said. But Staton, who moved to Florida three years ago, isn't planning to move back. The man who helped found Mad Dads in Omaha in 1989 said the faith-based crime-fighting organization has gotten a new lease on life in Jacksonville. Staton, 57, has gotten a new lease on life as well. "I love it there," he said.*

Did the reporter and Staton meet by coincidence? What was the purpose of this article? Why was it relevant for Staton to give his views on what is going on in Omaha when he did little to have an impact on crime when he and his organization were based here? Why no questions on the finances of his organization other than the donations? Why no questions about what happened to the donations he solicited while in Omaha? It's clear that the World-Herald views Staton as one of its "boys" in much the same way Hal Daub did. The facts speak for themselves.

The article continues:

> *His life has been a roller-coaster in the last three years. He beat kidney cancer in 2001. He married Omaha day-care provider Frankie Carter in 2002. And he moved*

> *Mad Dads from the city of its birth. Staton founded the organization 15 years ago with Bishop Robert Tyler and the late John Foster after Foster's son was beaten by a gang. The idea of black fathers taking to the streets to confront gangs and drugs immediately caught on. Just 10 months after the group's incorporation, the first President Bush named it one of his Thousand Points of light. In 1994, President Clinton presented Mad Dads with a volunteer action award.*

And as for that award, since Staton relocated to the state where Jeb Bush is Governor, it should not shock anyone to know that in October of 2002, Staton got more attention from another member of the Bush family – Columba, Jeb's wife. They announced a partnership, this time the organization working with the Florida Office of Drug Control! Staton, hobnobbing with people like Hal Daub and other racist Omahans, is clearly continuing his pattern of collusion down in Florida.

Like Cuba Gooding Jr., the "show-me-the-money" concept still appears to be the foundation of Staton's thinking. Check it out:

> *The organization now has 60 chapters in 16 states. Support in Omaha, however, waned. The Mad Dads board voted to relocate to Florida, where the organization has 30 chapters and has attracted the support of state and local government ... He [Staton] ... went full time with the organization last year after it received a $137,000 grant from the city. Mad Dads is hoping for $200,000 this year, he said. "Jacksonville," he said, "has had the foresight to see that services can't be left to United Way."*

Mo' money, mo' money mo' money. And crime hasn't dropped a single point since they've been in Jacksonville – just like it never budged (except to increase) while the self-named "Mad Dads" were here in the River City. The message is clear: talk loud and do nothing and you get paid; confront the system and its racism and you get "whitelisted."

It gets worse:

> *Staton's newest initiative is Black on Black Love – a campaign to reduce black-on-black crime. "If we're killing each other," he said, "you can't blame the white community for that." Staton said entertainer Bill Cosby's controversial criticism of underachieving blacks was*

"absolutely on target." He said he was disappointed with black leaders in Omaha who have excoriated Police Chief Thomas Warren for seeking DNA samples from black male employees at OPPD in an effort to solve the rapes of four black women. **He also labeled as pathetic the community response to the beating that led to the death of 16-year-old Chasity Wright on June 25 and the stabbing death five days later of 22-year-old Robert Everett. "There's no 'We've got to stop this,'" Staton said. "God's people in this city ought to be outraged** by what the devil is doing" (emphasis added).

Black on black love – and then he comes to Omaha and plays the role of the Uncle Tom? No one "blames" the white community for black on black crime; we are just waiting for them to accept responsibility for the snitch system they created which, in turn, places black youth against black youth and family against family in the name of "working off charges" and "downward departures."

Why would the reporter care about what Bill Cosby said and a black reaction? Because the World-Herald knows a "tom" when it sees one and they want to pit one black against another. They want to get Negroes to speak out against Senator Ernie Chambers. They want to divide-and-conquer, which they have done for decades. But those sorry hicks can't do anything unless we allow it: ***and there are too many of us staggering around here willing to play their sick game.***

Staton's views have no bearing on what goes on here. He played the role of the snitch back THEN, and he plays that role now. Why doesn't he fight white collar crime, the source behind the money that floods these communities with the drugs that the gangs then turn around and sell? Why doesn't he go after the kingpins? Florida has so much cocaine that more than 99% of its paper currency tests positive for cocaine powder! Where is the black version of Matlock THEN?

<u>1995 – Law Enforcement Sunday</u>

So considering the foolishness that exists on both sides of this argument, in all of their infinite wisdom and glory, neither can see the forest for the trees. The representatives of the black community, people who are trusted to protect the poor and neglected, all they can do is come up with this kind of idea: let's have a kiss-the cops'-ass ceremony. These are not their exact words of course, but that is just what they did. In front of everybody.

Sometimes an entire community gets in on the snitching. I'm not just talking about calling in to a phone number and "telling" so that you can get paid if what you tell leads to an arrest or conviction, I'm talking about an actual celebration of snitching, a celebration and homage to the very group of white men who have been gunning down black youth, harassing black women, engaging in illegal activity including smoking dope inside their cruisers at night and getting paid for it. I'm talking about a celebration of the Omaha Police Division.

That's what these black people in North Omaha did.

They called it "Law Enforcement Sunday," and check this out: the cops were asked to attend the church of their choice in full police uniform! Even guns! The purpose of the event? According to the World-Herald, "The day, to be observed this Sunday, is intended to improve the relationship between Omahans and law-enforcement officers." (James-Johnson, 1995: 15). All this took place on **Sunday, October 29, 1995**. These black people made all these statements, humbled themselves, and once again fell prey to the media's manipulated manifestations of reality.

> The Rev. Negil McPherson, president of the Interdenominational Ministerial Alliance, said all churches, synagogues and mosques in the Omaha area are encouraged to observe the day, regardless of their racial makeup. McPherson said there is a need to improve the relationship between law-enforcement officers and citizens throughout the community, not just among blacks. (James-Johnson, 1995: 25)

This is always the war cry of the bootlicker: "we must represent everyone, not just ourselves!' And when the dust clears, everybody else gets paid but us! Everybody else has rights but us! Everybody else is free but us! As Richard Pryor once asked, "How long is this bullshit gonna continya?" Meanwhile, McPherson keeps talking:

> He said the ministerial alliance is calling on law enforcement to do its part by eliminating officers who give law enforcement agencies a bad name. "I believe in every police department in this country there is a Mark Fuhrman," he said. "Mark Fuhrmans are in the minority, but if the others do not expose the Mark Fuhrmans, it

> makes the entire department look bad." . (James-Johnson, 1995: 9)

McPherson could not have been more wrong. Perhaps there should be a rule against speaking if you are ignorant of that subject. At any rate, there is no doubt that Furhman is not the exception, nor is his type in "the minority" among cops. The fact is, those who keep quiet are just as guilty as the ones who commit the crime. In my book, "silence is consent."

Also during "Law Enforcement Sunday, Chief Skinner had something to say:,

> " ... a large organization like a police department is always going to have some people who don't act as professionally as they should, but that shouldn't soil the reputation of the entire department. We've consistently taken steps to see that that type of person not become an Omaha police officer, or if we discover one in the department, we take very immediate and appropriate steps to deal with that person ... " . (James-Johnson, 1995: 9)

What lies. How can you screen racism when racism is the norm? The only reason the brothers and sisters who make the force are there is because they are so incredibly ethical and moral that the white man has no choice but to give them a shot! Meanwhile, a lot of these white cops have had their juvenile records expunged, but those are the times when their personalities were formed. More than a few made a racial remark to someone black and got their ass kicked. Now, armed with a badge, a gun and some mace, they can exact revenge on blacks, ANY black, in hopes of salvaging some semblance of self-esteem.

> As soldiers in the battle against violence and gang activity in Omaha, members of Grace Apostolic Church paused Sunday to pay tribute to one of their fellow warriors -- Omaha Police Chief James Skinner. (James-Johnson, 1995: 9)

Say what? Let's read on:

> The Rev. William D. Barlowe, pastor of the church, set the stage with an introduction about the need for the community and the Police Department to work together. He described Skinner and the church as "members of the

> same team" and encouraged the congregation to make the
> police chief feel welcome. . (James-Johnson, 1995: 9)

Remember that description folks: Skinner and the church, according to Rev. Barlowe, are "members of the same team." I didn't say it – he did. Back to the feel-good day for the cops:

> With that, most of the 500 people in the audience jumped
> to their feet to give Skinner a standing ovation. Skinner,
> when he reached the lectern, was speechless for a
> moment. "You have humbled me," he said. "You've very
> much overwhelmed me." . (James-Johnson, 1995: 9)

Humbled? If black people were in a position to humble him, wouldn't he have been more responsive from the get-go? To be "humbled" means to "cause to be unpretentious." Was Skinner pretentious from the outset? Maybe he was, maybe he wasn't. But one thing is for sure: coming into a church with a gun on your hip is no way to show how "humbled" you have become, now is it?

Check out what Muldoon was doing on the other side of town:

> Sgt. William Muldoon, spokesman for the Police
> Department, was in uniform at Sacred Heart Catholic
> Church, 2218 Binney St. He was accompanied by his 10-
> year-old daughter, Regina. During the Sign of Peace
> about a dozen people congregated around him to shake
> his hand. "The Spirit was here today," Muldoon said after
> Mass. "People were so warm it made me feel like part of
> the community." . (James-Johnson, 1995: 9)

Muldoon admits he feels no connection, although most of you would consider what he said a compliment. What he said was, "The spirit was here today … People were so warm it made me feel like part of the community." He should have already felt that way because North Omaha IS part of the Omaha community. But when a person is racist, his words often condemn him. In this case, it is clear that Muldoon sees himself as "a man apart" from the black community because he, Muldoon, is white. Car 54 – where are you?

Back to Bishop Barlowe and the collective belief by those present that the cops are our pals:

> [Barlowe] ... said law enforcement and the community have to work together if progress is to be made in the fight against gangs and violence. "We need as a church to let law enforcement know that we as a community need you, not only to protect us but protect our children," He said to Skinner, his words interrupted by a standing ovation. "We don't need to look at law enforcement as an adversary, and because it happened in North Omaha, we don't want law enforcement to look at us as the adversary. We're on the same team." . (James-Johnson, 1995: 11)

We are not on the same team with the police department. We are not even on the field. We are in the back of the locker room, scrubbing the floors. And yet the one who are "players" – the cops themselves – are so racist that they are not satisfied with not having you on the field or in the stands. They wait until a time-out or half time and then come into the locker room where you labor away, and then commence to beating the shit out of you just for laughs. This is the way it is in Omaha, and the "officials," "referees," "line judges," "back judges" and the Commissioner are all the same race as the "players." So guess what the finding is? "No harm, no foul."

> Several church members said after the service that they believed Skinner's visit to the church was a step in the right direction for the community and the Police Department. Clyde Comer Jr., 36, said he saw Skinner outside and the chief came up him and shook his hand. "I didn't see a uniform. I saw a man approaching me with his hand out," Comer said. "We need more of that. He could've walked right by me, but he didn't. He came outside of himself for a moment just to say hi." . (James-Johnson, 1995: 11)

Somebody said that Skinner's visit was a step I the right direction for the community and the police department. That is why history is so important: it rewards our research, as Malcolm taught. And what do we find now, almost a full decade later?

The same old thang.

2004

The year 2004 brings us to the end of this longitudinal examination. We end with speeches from two men: one, a Black state senator with more than three and a half decades in the Nebraska Unicameral and the other, also Black, a newly elected police chief for the Omaha Police Department.

The latter appointment and accomplishment, history making in itself, would be a cause for rejoicing were it not for the facts presented by the previous elected official.

Senator Chambers Speech on DNA Collection and Community Rights

At an August 21 community meeting, Senator Chambers made an important speech about the police, DNA and community rights. A key part of that speech follows:

> "… So with all of these admissions, he's the kind of man that the County Attorney uses to try to get somebody convicted. And it's the same Stu Dornan who spoke after Albert Rucker was killed, and talked about these individuals who commit all these crimes and continue to be allowed to run around on the street. Well, after he – as County Attorney – condemned THAT situation in Rucker's case, is using an individual who has numerous felonies to rat out somebody else.
>
> But if I had not gotten that bill through the Legislature – and it was a FIGHT – this stuff on the snitches would not come out. The bill says, simply, that a jail house snitch who is going to be used, must provide information – meaning the County Attorney must – any convictions, any statements he's given in the past, any statements that he's given that he recanted, or he took back, any statements that were found to be false – anything in his background that could reflect on his credibility. The prosecutors used to bring these people up and didn't have to say any of that."
>
> Without fighting bills -- the County Attorney's were against it, some of the Senators were against it. You all don't realize the kind of representative you've got down there. Another incident in the paper describes some innocent third party victims of a police chase, given a combined total of one-point-five million dollars. It's less than what the injuries justify, but again, that's because of a bill that I fought through the Legislature. Overcame the Chief, the police officers, mayor, other senators, to point out that police chases are going to occur, and society

approves of this method of law enforcement, when an innocent third-party is hurt or injured, it's society's responsibility to make that person whole to the extent that money can.

So, there is what is known as strict liability. The agency that hires the cops, whether it's the city, the county or the state – that agency must respond in damages, to the innocent third-party who is hurt. Maybe that doesn't resonate with too many people in this room, but you never know when some of these crazy cops are going to be having somebody flying down 24th, 42nd, 30th, or any other street, and you or a family member will be a victim.

At that time you won't know whose protective arms were spread over you, you won't know in whose good hands you were, but you'll thank whatever god you worship that there's something in the law that says you can get some amount of money for the injuries that you've suffered.

Now what I have here – I'm not going to take them all out – these letters represent about a month of mail that I get. And these are letters that I haven't even gone into yet. Haven't even responded to them. I get briefs, I get court transcripts, all kinds of complaints: domestic problems, police problems, housing, schools – everything. I try to help people wherever I can, but remember: you're looking at one man. The mayor has a staff, other people have staffs. And some of them refer these cases to me.

People will call me with a problem, and I will work on it. And once it's resolved, they won't tell me that it was resolved even. And I'm carrying it around in my head thinking that the next shoe is going to drop then I'm going to have to do something else. Then, something will bring us in contact and they'll say, 'oh by the way, that problem was solved.' And I say, "I wish you would have let me know, I could have let that go.'

When people send me things, and I say I'll get to them when can, that sounds cold to the individual who is coming to me. But in the same what that that person has a pressing problem, wants me to drop everything for them, they must realize that there are literally hundreds of other whose problems are on my desk, or table, on the floor in my office. If you ever came down to Lincoln, you'd wonder why I don't go crazy. But I try to wade through that stuff and do with it what I can, when I get to it.

I know that we're discussing a concern about very serious problems that brought us here today. Even with that being the case, I've got to maintain my priorities. I'm what the Bible refers to as a man who is faithful in season, and out of season. I'm the only Senator who, when we're not in session, will still be there every day. Who, in session, will be there every day. I go there weekends, holidays – because there are people whose problems don't stop for the weekends or the holidays. But when other people are enjoying their families, or going on vacation, just kicking back and taking it easy, should realize that there's at least one person who's working all of the time.

Everybody takes a break – except me. And I'm not saying it for sympathy, but to make you all understand that as serious as the problems are that you bring to me, there are other things that I'm working on.

I have to prepare for a hearing that's coming up Thursday, to try to open records on these DNA racial profiling sweeps. Now, there are many black lawyers in the city – they're not doing it. Fortunately, one of the men has a white lawyer, Bill Gallup, and I sent him some information and talked to the man who was unjustifiably subjected to a Court order to take him to jail and make him give a sample. So Gallup is going to be at that hearing. He filed a motion to unseal the records. I wrote a 12-page memorandum – which some people would call a legal brief – to get this judge to see that that information should be open.

What I want to see the affidavit or the sworn statement of the cops that led the judge to issue that order. I also want to see the affidavit of the cops that led the judge to issue what is called a general warrant to search the personnel records of OPPD to get all of the information on all the black employees. That warrant is illegal on its face! The law does not allow general warrants, and to make it simple, that means a blanket kind of warrant where you don't describe anybody precisely enough, so that the cop serving it will not use it to catch an innocent person.

So when they talk about somebody between 175 and 250 pounds, between 25 and 40 years old, who was bald, but they go after men with dreadlocks, who has a big stomach but they go after men who are frailer than I am, it's clear that they are using a general warrant – something that allows them to racially profile all the black men in this community. See, because black is a term that doesn't relate to complexion – this man sitting in the front row who probably is Caucasian – if one of his parents were black and he came out looking that white, he would fit under that description, because they don't say 'a black person, dark complexion, medium complexion, brown, light brown' – just the term, black.

Is Whoopi Goldberg black? Is she? (laughter) I'm talking about complexion. What about Halle Berry? (audience: "Black") Mariah Carey? (audience: "Black"). So the thing is, we have three black women. That doesn't let you know ANYTHING about what their complexion is.

I'm not wasting time, it might seem like it because I'm not dealing directly right away with what I came here for, but to show you how broad our problems are, and that I'm addressing those. There are a lot of you all who work on these problems. But the ones I deal with are only me. While I'm working on THESE, there's nobody addressing those that I have to deal with. Just keep that in mind.

Now, what I'm going to do is contact the Chief Justice and tell him about the way the courts are allowing cases to go forward on the word of snitches alone; no corroborating evidence, and they're not requiring the County Attorney, or the City Prosecutor – if he begins to do that – to bring forth any physical evidence or even strong circumstantial evidence.

This person that the articles are about, that I mentioned who is snitching, said that he overheard a conversation in 1999; between two guys in Chicago, arguing. When he faces all these charges, he'll say anything. Matthew put a good column in the Omaha Star this week. If you are facing what looks like humongus time, and all you have to do is lie on somebody else or rat on them. And if you're lucky like this guy, you'll be paid and they'll ship you someplace and give you rent and utilities, who in this room would not rat? I don't want you to raise your hand, maybe you wouldn't, but I want you to get the point and the picture of how they're laying this stuff out.

So, they will get all these guys who are locked up and make it clear, all you've got to do is snitch; I mean get on the witness stand – stick with that lie! Do like the cops do who took Lying 101. If Jesus and the angels come down and say you're lying, you say, 'No, I'm not.'

And try to look innocent, try to look sincere, and like this guy: "Yes, I've lied before. I've committed felonies before. I've committed crimes of dishonesty. I've stolen checks. I fraudulently established a bank account, then I fraudulently withdrew that money which came from these stolen checks. All those things I did. I've lied to the police, gave them false information. Then when they came to get me, I took off running. But as you can see, I'm not in the best of shape, and they caught me. I admit all that. I'm not here saying I'm a good person. I'm not saying that I haven't done anything wrong. But anybody can change, and in this instance, the crime was so horrendous, that if you don't believe anything else that I say, you should believe me this time."

They teach 'em that! And if it's a white jury dealing with a black man – they don't care about us, anyway – "we can get one of them off the street even if we think he didn't do what they accuse him of, and we'll let this go, who'll worked in our cause, some more, someplace else."

There are some complaints, by some federal judges, that state cases – not just in Nebraska – are being turned into Federal cases because under the Federal law there are some things that they can do to mess over somebody's rights which cannot be done under state law. So they have an array of promises they can make. If you snitch, I will not prosecute you for the offenses you committed. And you say, "I'm not a snitch." "Okay, you don't want to snitch, then we're going to put you over in the Federal system. And we're going to guarantee you time so long, and if you put on binoculars you won't see the end of it. (Laughter) And if that time we're going to give you was stretched out like a highway, you'd see the curve of the Earth (laughter) before you see the end of that time. And you're going to do every day of it because there's no parole in the Federal system.

Now – and then they'll tell you, "so what if somebody lies on you?" See, white people know how bad the system is, and those are the times they admit it. You think a white jury is gonna believe YOU? "I'm a FEDERAL prosecutor, I'm the GOVERNMENT. This is the government of the United States of America against a black criminal – who's out there dealing drugs, probably selling guns, undermining the community.

And then they say some things in such a way that white people KNOW: "he's talking about THEM."

They're not limited by their neighborhood; they don't respect ANYBODY. That's when the white people know, "he's talking about THEM." So again, white people say, "well, send him away – doesn't make me any difference."

But then, there's something we have to start telling young black men – and some of the older ones. Big drug dealers don't get caught. You know why they don't get caught? Because they dress like ordinarily people, they might have a job of some kind, they have a family, they want their kids to go to school, they want to be respectable and respected, and they don't drive a car that's about three inches off the street with those mag tires and rims. They don't walk weighted down by a whole lot of jewelry and wearing these funny clothes and in some cases hanging off their rear end. You know what these fools are telling the white man? The one who WANTS to get 'em? "Hey man, I'm a drug dealer, come get ME." Then, once they get 'em, the come crying.

I believe the law has to be fair to everybody and by that I mean applied in the same way to people who are similarly situated, without regard to race. But we know that that's not going to be the case. So what these black men need to realize – and some women are getting caught in it. I don't know if this one in Lincoln that I read about this morning, got about eleven years for selling crack. They need to be told that: "you are mortgaging you future."

Suppose you sell dope and you wind up with three hundred thousand dollars, and that boggles your mind; buy all these cars and funny clothes and waste your money and walk around here clanking with all this jewelry like --- well, like somebody wearing tin cans and walking through a junkyard in a hurricane. Clanking everywhere you go, and thinking people's – saying, "look at me" – but you don't know WHO'S looking at you and for what purpose.

So you got the $300,000 and they give you 30 years. If you divide 300,000 by 30, that comes out to ten thousand dollars. You're going to give up a year of your life for ten thousand dollars? That's less than I make in the Legislature and I don't make minimum wage. We have to get people to think and don't create bigger problems than we already have.

Drugs are devastating our community, and people who are selling drugs are allowed to do it in our community. But when the law enforcement people have to make it look like they're doing something about crime, they've got a ready-made group of victims that they can go after. You know why I say victims? Because the law is not going to apply to them as it does to everybody else.

If I know that somebody is dealing drugs, and I go tell the man this man is dealing drugs, that should not be enough to convict that person. Conduct is criminal only because the law makes it so. And at the same time the law makes it a crime, the Constitution and the law establish the standard that has to be met before society can convict this person and punish this person for having engaged in this conduct.

So if you're going to be charged with violating one of society's laws or rules, those who are going to get you have to be required to follow the rules that are in place for them to CONVICT you. Nothing is a crime because god said it is! Something is a crime in this state only because the LEGISLATURE said that it is, and that's the way it is in EVERY state. And that same Legislature said you can not engage in unreasonable searches and seizures. You have to have probably cause before you search a person, you have to have probably cause before you search somebody's house, their papers, their effects, or anything else.

And when you get a warrant, a warrant can be issued only when there is probable cause to believe that the person who is the target has committed a crime. And if you're getting the warrant to search premises, there has to be probable cause that evidence of a crime will be found at that location. The law says that. Sometimes some of us get so upset and carried away with how angry we are at people accused of crimes that we say "throw the book away" and "throw the book at 'em." "Don't let 'em get away."

Well, if they haven't done the kind of thing that the law can get 'em for, let 'em get away. Let 'em go. And if they're doing these things, and I'm a smart cop – and to be a smart cop, with due respect to my black brothers who are cops y'all know who I'm talking about – you don't have to be too bright. I'd say "now wait a minute. He's been dealing drugs for thirty years. I know what I'll do: I'll WATCH him! And I'll catch him doing it. Then, when I catch him, I've got the evidence."

They know how to catch somebody if the WANT to, because they've caught people that they don't prosecute. They've got a stable of snitches. And if I'm a homicide detective, I'll let a drug dealer go if he'll snitch for me, and if I'm a narcotics officer, I'll let a killer go if he'll snitch for ME! So the killers go, the drug dealers go – how do you think some of these guys when they finally get caught, have ALL of these have all of these heavy crimes that were charged against them? Where plea bargains were entered and charges were dropped? Where they were put on probation? When somebody who works every day and went afoul of the law for the first time they committed a crime they might get three years in the pen – why is that? Because of what the system is doing.

Now I wanted to give a context in which to make a suggestion, because I've got my eye on that clock back there.

What I think we're going to have to try to do is continue putting together information about the things that are being done with these snitches, and families and individuals who have been harassed and hounded by this cop, Jeff Gasaway. I've told the Mayor about him, and that I'm going to get information from people who have complaints. So people who have information about Gasaway, send it to me, and date it. I did get some packets of letters from people who are now locked up, and some people who are not, but none of them is dated. They can still be of value, but if it's dated, its better.

I also think we should put forth an effort – and when I say "we", I'm willing to work hard on this – I'll talk first to the U.S. Attorney for the Nebraska District, Mike Heavican, about the way they're using these snitches, and that's the only kind of evidence they've got. And they're using the threat of converting a State case into a Federal case to coerce people into snitching, knowing that the snitch is a liar. And see, they would not accept what this snitch would say against a white person.

And if he will NOT do anything about what has become a pattern, then for whatever it's worth, a contact will be to the U.S. Department of Justice, and I will contact Hagel and Ben Nelson, U.S. Senators and a Congressperson. And when they don't do anything as I know they won't, I will make contact with some of the other U.S. Senators who are Democrats on the Senate Judiciary Committee, and if there are any on the House Judiciary Committee, those too.

There are some individuals, in Congress, who MIGHT take an interest. But it would be better to touch base with the local Senators – by local I mean those from

THIS state who are sitting in Washington, first. And I'm willing to do that. But I want information, in my hand, that I can share with them, so that they're not able to say what they always want to say, "This is Chambers who has a grudge against the police." Now, those are the things that I am willing to do. But I want some information. I will talk to the U.S. Attorney, I will contact the two U.S. Senators and the three members of the House of Representatives. Doug Bereuter is still there, and he's the one who came out, in writing, against the war in Iraq.

If THAT fails, as it likely will, I will see if anybody in the Justice Department will take an interest, and if any U.S. Senators or House members will take an interest. And the more information that I have, the better it will be. Matthew is going to work on this project with me – he didn't know that, but he knows it now – he said that whatever I need him for, he'll be there, and there are things that he can do that would take some of that legwork off of me, and help with the writing and other things. He has seen some of the work that I've produced – thick documents and you know how they get typed? By me. Seriously. I've typed briefs, single spaced, fifty pages.

How many hours are there in a day? Well, twenty-four. How many hours can a man work? Maybe sixteen. But the devil never sleeps." (Laughter and applause).

A Speech by African-American Police Chief Thomas Warren

On the same day – August 21, 2004 -- also at the invitation of Mothers and Families Against Conspiracy, Police Chief Thomas Warren spoke. Following are his words about his "role" as a police officer and the fact that he is not about to compromise it for anyone. He was the leader of an otherwise racist police force and though black, was as "anti-black" as any police chief before him. My analyses of his words will filter in and out. The implication of his speech and the long-time application of his actions to the black community shows that Warren has always been snitch material. My emphases in bold-face will bear this out.

In vintage "house negro" fashion, Warren's presentation begins:

> Good morning. I appreciate the invitation to visit. I did receive a letter and correspondence and had a chance to visit with Miss Shaw briefly. I kind of wanted to **set**

some ground rules in terms of why I'm here and what I can offer in terms of maybe explaining why we do what we do. But at the same time, answer the questions that you may have.

Certainly I represent law enforcement and I received a letter and it contained a number of allegations and a number of assertions. As I mentioned to Miss Shaw, we may not agree on a lot of things, but I'm compelled and obligated to address your concerns if you feel that there's been officer misconduct.

What we are dealing with though, is a *system*. And of course, my role in this system is representing law enforcement and law enforcement's interests. I was born and raised in this community, so I understand what the issues are, the concerns are, of the residents of this community. Prior to my appointment as Chief of Police, I was precinct commander of the Northeast Precinct for the last two years. I can tell you without any reservation, what my objectives, my priorities were. And that was to reduce gun violence, to reduce gang activity and to reduce drug distribution. **And so understand my role, and that is that of law enforcement**. And my role is to arrest individuals who break the law, the prosecutor's job is to try those individuals, and convict them. And it is the judiciary's responsibility to sentence those individuals. So we may have different perspectives. But I'm sensitive to the issues that have been presented and discussed, understand my role.

Certainly, I'm very respectful of your perspectives, and I only ask that while we may disagree, our disagreements be respectful. So with that, I'll tell you that dealing with dope dealing and gang banging and that kind of activity is very, very serious business. Very, very dangerous. And it's our approach to use every legal tactic to address these problems because I am genuinely concerned about the well-being of the citizens of Omaha, particularly the citizens of North Omaha, because we have to deal with issues of gun violence and gang banging.

When we talk about this type of activity, many of the individuals are synonymous. We have gang banging drug dealers who get engaged in acts of gun violence. And it is our strategy to utilize those legal tactics, **and we have partnered with the United States Attorney's office under the Project Safe Neighborhoods program**, because some of the difficulties that we encounter when we investigate these types of offenses is the lack of cooperation. The lack of cooperation sometimes of victims, the lack of cooperation from witnesses, and I can tell you that we do rely on that gun charge.

Oftentimes where we'll investigate a homicide or a felony assault, or destruction of property of an occupied dwelling, commonly referred to as a drive by shooting, we may not get that level of cooperation necessary in order to effectively prosecute a case. So we do rely oftentimes on that gun charge when we have a situation where someone may be in possession of an illegal firearm, whether its stolen or faced, a short shotgun. If it fits the criteria for prosecution in Federal court, we'll submit that case to the United States Attorneys office. If it's a matter of a person who is illegally in possession of a firearm, and it's a companion charge, whether its possession with intent to deliver a narcotic -- crack cocaine, for example -- and it fits the criteria for Federal court, then we'll submit that case to the United States Attorneys office because we know the sanctions are much more severe. That's our role, reducing crime, reducing crime and violence, and that's my objective.

I am concerned about the law abiding citizens in this community, who want to live in the sanctity of their homes, and what we've seen recently, and particularly in northeast and southeast Omaha, are these incidents of gun violence, where innocent people are being hurt. We've seen incidents of gun violence where 10-year-olds, 12-year-olds, have been injured. And I know that many of these individuals involved in drug distribution and the gang banging perpetuate, perpetrate these crimes.

And so we try to utilize appropriate legal tactics to effectively investigate these cases, and when we have probably cause for arrest, we effect the arrest and **during the course of these investigations we do develop other information**. And when we're dealing with drug distribution in particular, by law, if two or more parties are engaged in activity for the purpose of creating a criminal enterprise, that's a conspiracy. We'll charge the evidence. We recognize that there is a significant amount of drug distribution that takes place in this community, we recognize that there is a significant amount of drug consumption that takes place in this community, and it has affected the lives of many people; It has affected families, both those individuals who are engaged in that practice in terms of distribution, as well as families of individuals who may be addicted to those substances, and it has had an adverse affect on our community.

And so our role, my role in terms of providing leadership to a law enforcement agency is to focus our attention on these priorities. Because if you feel that it doesn't have an effect on our community, a POSITIVE effect in terms of reducing crime and violence, from what we've seen here in the Northeast precinct, there's been a significant reduction in the overall crime rate. We've seen a significant reduction in incidents of gun violence in terms of volume. We have seen instances occur, but for example "shots fired calls for service" are down over 20 percent in Northeast precinct compared to same time frame last year. And what that represents is a potential homicide, a potential felony assault or a potential destruction of property of an occupied dwelling.

And so I know that our strategies have had a positive effect on our community in terms of making this community safer. That's my role. And so, I'll address your questions and concerns in regards to our tactics. I know there are concerns with regard to utilization of proffers, co-defendants. But you recognize, too, that when you're dealing with individuals who are engaged in dealing illegal drugs, unless they manufacture the product themselves, or sell and distribute the product themselves, they are generally in cahoots with someone, and typically, if individuals are charged, and arrested, subject to prosecution, **there may be a willingness on the part of that individual to cooperate with law enforcement authorities.**

> **This cooperation *has* to be voluntary, it cannot be coerced, by law**. And, of course, there's all types of public perspectives on that approach and utilization of these tactics, but there are safeguards built into the system and certainly in terms of making sure that cases are prosecuted properly and individual's rights are not being violated. There are individuals who represent the interests of criminal defendants, and that's what they get paid for.
>
> And so, I'm not here to discuss guilt or innocence of any particular defendant. I'll try to describe what we do and I'll try to describe why we do it in a very general sense. Understand what my role is and again, **I don't really compromise on that perspective.**

Warren had to threaten to sue when the department tried to bypass him for the Chief position even though he outscored everyone else. So they handed it over begrudgingly. He didn't care. He wanted to be head nigger in charge and that's what they made him. They still had their way and he kowtowed to most of the concerns of the white-led police union. The only thing that changed from his serving as police chief and the white boys who served before him was that he made things WORSE for North Omaha. While boasting of having been there, look at what he did when he got a little power.

In March of 2015 Warren was honored by Congress "For his leadership and service in Omaha."

Today in Omaha, young black men continued to tell on each other and, as a result, more of their friends got locked up and received incredible amounts of prison time, usually in the area of 10-35 years. Some young men stood strong. But in all cases, the black mothers rose to the occasion.

CONCLUSION

Snitching is as American as apple pie. The heroes of film and television, masquerading under the guise of "law enforcement," are really nothing more than undercover agents – snitches. Their job is to betray, infiltrate and tell everything they know. Their job is to take loyalty to one side, win their trust and then testify against them if and when the case gets to court.

In the halls of Washington, DC political leaders rely on and read reports filed by "Confidential informants" who are at work all over the world. In almost every country around the globe there are what have been called spies. There are activities referred to as "espionage." All of this is about snitching so that America can gain an advantage over it's "opposition."

On the streets the cops are so buffoonish that they have to rely on the public to find out which way is up. With the help of the media, they have to offer up "rewards" for tips that lead to arrests and convictions.

When I was coming up we were told as children that if we saw something, tell an adult. But as I grew up the code of the street changed that order to "don't snitch" and more recently, "snitches get stitches." And so it has come to pass with one informant, Whitey Bulger.

In October of 2018, one of the government's biggest snitches was killed while in prison. The following news story, written by Larry McShane of the *New York Daily News*, appeared under the headline, "Boston mob boss Whitey Bulger killed in West Virginia prison."

According to the article,

> Notorious Boston mob boss James (Whitey) Bulger was killed Tuesday inside a West Virginia federal prison, according to various reports. **The 89-year-old Irish-American gangster** was only **transferred one day earlier** to the high-security prison in Hazelton, W. Va., where officials initially reported an inmate was slain overnight. (McShane, 2018)

Those inmates were waiting on Whitey's ass. They knew he was coming and probably got the intel from a prison guard. They gave the word and then turned the other way while the "hit" was carried out. How else to explain it? It's a high security prison and he was killed right away. Somebody got paid, and more likely than not the people who handled the transfer papers (and probably the warden and the government) were all a part of the deal.

Continuing:

> Bulger was later identified as the dead man, although officials **released no details surrounding his sudden, shocking and violent demise**. Bulger, previously held in Florida, was convicted of 11 murders himself during his bloody reign as crime boss in his hometown of Boston. The federal Bureau of Prisons did not return a call and an email for confirmation. Hazelton is home to about 1,300 inmates. (McShane, 2018)

Maybe the body wasn't Bulger's. Maybe it was somebody else and they switched bodies to relocate Whitey once again. Who knows – the U.S. government is criminal in its own right. Now everybody things Whitey is dead, which is the same outcome as the Witness Protection Program: they eliminate identity and the people who were snitched on simply give up.

> Bulger spent 16 years on the FBI's Most Wanted list after going on the lam, fleeing his hometown as the feds closed in. He was busted in 2011 in California and convicted two years later for an assortment of crimes including the homicides. **His legend only grew as Bulger evaded arrest after his disappearance,** with endless reported sightings around the U.S. and the world. One tipster insisted spying Bulger inside a Boston movie theater in 2006, watching the Martin Scorsese movie "The Departed" — where Jack Nicholson played a mob boss based on the fugitive son of South Boston.(McShane, 2018 – emphasis added)

He made money, he got away with murder after murder, he humiliated the judicial system and he embarrassed the FBI time and time again. All of these are motives for the government to step in and make his "disappearance" as permanent as possible. As a snitch he had done his job, and keeping him alive only further jeopardized his arrest because he might talk or cut some other kind of deal for a book or movie. Such a chance could not be taken.

So be it an Irish mobster, an Italian gangster or a black drug dealer – the U.S. government has always had snitches galore on a number of levels. This book is written to serve as a primer, a seed so that you, the reader, will care enough to engage in additional research, work and study on how such a system of confidential informants, tattle tales, snitches, canaries and outright sellouts can continue to be used as a "tool of law enforcement." And what makes it worse is that once the "contract" is agreed upon, these same law enforcement people USE that confidential informant status to control and continue to manipulate the snitch. In far too many cases this had led to black-on-black murders.

The saying on the street is that "snitches get stitches." But before they decide to turn evidence on their comrades and give up what they know, there is another factor that is involved: "snitches get riches."

REFERENCES

Anthony, Earl (1970) *Picking Up the Gun: a report on the Black Panthers*. New York, New York: The Dial Press.

Anthony, Earl (1989) *Spitting in the Wind: The True Story Behind the Violent Legacy of the Black Panther Party*. Santa Monica, California: Roundtable Publishers.

Brown, Elaine. *A Taste of Power: A Black Woman's Story*. New York, New York: Anchor Books.

Fields, Suzanne. (2018, January 17) Vindication for a Whistleblower. Washington Times. Retrieved from https://www.washingtontimes.com/news/2018/jan/17/20-years-on-linda-tripp-gets-the-last-laughs-at-th/

Sabia, Carmine (2016, January 16). Linda Tripp says she exposed Monica Lewinsky's affair because her life was 'in danger' – she feared an 'accident'. *Business and Politics Review*. Retrieved from https://www.bizpacreview.com/2016/01/18/linda-tripp-says-she-exposed-monica-lewinskys-affair-because-her-life-was-in-danger-she-feared-an-accident-296010

Cganemccalla (2011, June 24). Top 5 Notorious Gangsters Turned Informants. TV News One. Retrieved from https://newsone.com/760535/top-5-gangsters-turned-informants/

ESPN.com (2008, October 21). Canseco Regrets Naming Names in His Book About Steroids. Retrieved from http://www.espn.com/mlb/news/story?id=3655031

Hancock, David (2005, February 10). Slugger Tells 60 Minutes He Injected Mark McGwire, Others. CBS News. Retrieved from https://www.cbsnews.com/news/steroid-user-canseco-names-names/

Levine, Michael (2009). "The Weakest Link: The Dire Consequences of a Weak Link in the Informant Handling and Covert Operations Chain-of-Command". *Law Enforcement Executive Forum*,

McShane, Larry (2018, October 30). Boston mob boss Whitey Bulger killed in West Virginia prison. *New York Daily News*. Retrieved from http://www.nydailynews.com/news/crime/ny-metro-white-bulger-dead-prison-20181030-story.html

Mental Floss (2008, August 2) 6 Historical Snitches (Who Weren't Named Judas). Retrieved from http://mentalfloss.com/article/19243/6-historical-snitches-who-werent-named-judas

Piazza, Jo (2008, June 23). Shaq: Kobe Bryant ruined my marriage. *Daily News*. Retrieved from http://www.nydailynews.com/entertainment/gossip/shaq-kobe-bryant-ruined-marriage-article-1.297264

Ranker (2018) The Best Rappers Named After Gangsters. Retrieved from https://www.ranker.com/list/rappers-named-after-gangsters-and-criminals/ranker-hip-hop

Shelton, Jacob (2015). Infamous Snitches Who Avoided Life in Prison. Ranker. Retrieved from https://www.ranker.com/list/famous-snitches/jacob-shelton

Smassaro (2018). The Mafia Blog. Retrieved from http://mafialifeblog.com/omertacode-of-silence%E2%80%9Che-who-is-deaf-blind-and-silent-will-live-a-hundred-years-in-peace/

"Sociology of Confinement: Assimilation and the Prison 'Rat'" by EH Johnson. *The Journal of Criminal Law, Criminology, and Police Science*. 1961

"The Weakest Link: The Dire Consequences of a Weak Link in the Informant Handling and Covert Operations Chain-of-Command" by M Levine. *Law Enforcement Executive Forum*, 2009

Wold, Nathan (2015, February 17). 10 Of The Worst Snitches Of All Time. Listverse.com. Retrieved from https://listverse.com/2015/02/17/10-of-the-worst-snitches-of-all-time/

www.ingramcontent.com/pod-product-compliance
Lightning Source LLC
Chambersburg PA
CBHW062322220526
45469CB00008B/2597